THIS IS FOR
KATIE

THIS IS FOR
KATIE

Katie Snow

ISBN: 978-1-913590-24-6 Ebook
ISBN: 978-1-913590-23-9 Paperback

The Unbound Press
www.theunboundpress.com

This is for Katie...
because she asked me to.

CONTENTS

Hello, Katie

My name isn't Katie. Your name *might* be Katie. Maybe your name isn't Katie, but chances are, you know a girl named Katie. At the end of the day, it doesn't matter what your name is because, if you've ever dated a man and you're a woman, at one time or another, you've probably been a Katie.

So, who is Katie? Well, Katie is a girl looking for love. She knows it's out there but somehow, even inside of some of her long-term or committed relationships with men, it eludes her. Love feels just out of reach no matter who she meets or what choices she makes. She feels frustrated. She's an optimist. But, sometimes, Katie wants to give up.

Katie has a habit of standing her ground— and then maybe regretting it—because, oops, there she went again, choosing herself over that shitty relationship. Katie is a woman who gives respect, but she also expects it to be given. She wants to speak her truth and live in integrity, but she hasn't figured out why that doesn't work with the guys she likes. Katie hates games; however, sometimes she plays them anyway because she thinks she has to. *Isn't that what everyone else does?*

She has been told, but doesn't *quite* believe, that a man is going to magically save her. Despite aching for love and a romantic relationship, Katie has a feeling that what society, the movies, and maybe even her own mother are telling her don't completely make sense. She's actually a bit scared of that feeling. "What if it's true?" she wonders. "What if what I'm looking for isn't something a man can give me?" She tells herself and her friends, especially after she's been hurt, that she's done with men!! "Who needs them?!! They're all terrible." Then, usually in a week or less, she does a 180 and instructs her brain to *"Shut the fuck up!"* Katie goes right back to searching because if she doesn't get a ring or have a wedding—or, at the very least a guy who can accompany her to dinner and parties—then she's someone who is seen as unworthy by everyone, especially herself.

How can she be worthy if a guy hasn't chosen her? Oh, she'll never really admit to believing that last statement, but there's a devil on her shoulder who never turns her loose from that thought.

What if I told you some of the things Katie thinks are correct? A lot of other people, mostly women, will judge her as unworthy or having something wrong with her if she doesn't have a man. These women might actually be unhappy themselves, but they'll project that shit onto Katie anyway. Some of them are angry at Katie because she's free, but that's another story. Does the fact that she's still alone mean she's unworthy? No. Can Katie feel worth with or without a man? Absolutely. And that's the secret sauce to having everything she wants, including that great guy she fucking deserves. The only difference is that Katie has to get to a point where she doesn't see him as a goal. She has to see him as a person, no different from herself. He's not magical. He's not perfect. He's not going to give her a dream life...that's something she has to give herself. He's the icing on *her* cake. She baked the cake, he didn't.

This book was written for an *actual* Katie, just as the title states. She's a gorgeous girl who once worked for me and, while she did, Katie and I became unusually close. She gave me access into the intimate world of a young woman in search of a partner. She's also the girl who convinced me to create this book because she strongly felt that I had obtained way too much information about the opposite sex, and just about life in general, not to share it with other women like her. As a matter of fact, Katie once told me that she kept my raw manuscript with her for a period of time—before she *finally* landed in the relationship she wanted—and even made a few of her friends read it. More about my Katie in a bit.

You might be asking yourself the following right about now: "If this chick isn't named Katie then why in the hell does this book say it's written by Katie Snow?!!" Well, beautiful, if I used my actual name then how could I tell these stories, which are mostly about men whom I've dated and some of whom I continue to have friendships with and love for, and feel as though I had protected my own privacy and theirs? The answer is, I couldn't. Secondly, I realized while writing this book that I wasn't just writing it for Katie; I was also writing it to the younger, less experienced version of myself. I got to know her better. Writing to her made me love her (me) more. Through writing this book I learned how to forgive her for some of the mistakes I thought she had made. I also realized that she was strong and resilient and kind of brave for having taken all the chances she had in love. Essentially, I learned to appreciate the girl I had been and the woman I am now. The part of me who is, and has been, a Katie, has gotten me here. I owe her. She's a survivor and also the reason I have an amazing life.

Everything—other than my name—in this book is absolutely true. Well, it's my version of the truth. I think we all know that the opposite sex usually has a very different idea of what the truth is than we do.

Now, actual Katie is in her late twenties and I'm in my early forties. All of this started when I began observing her dating behavior and giving her advice. She was reading and referencing books that were written when I was her age! I couldn't believe it. In my opinion, those books weren't helpful even then, before cell phones and social media. *Who are the women who wrote that shit (Yes, sorry not sorry, I'm calling it shit.) anyway? Do we even know?!! Do we want their lives? And, well, who the fuck are they to try to set rules for us? I mean, seriously.* I'm a rebel and, as far as I'm concerned, as the cliché goes: "Rules are bullshit." Oops, what I meant was, "Rules are meant to be broken."

I was left totally perplexed by the lack of communication and general confusion that women in their twenties, including Katie, were exhibiting with men. We're on the heels of one of the most powerful moments in female history, and I *still* see women objecti-fying themselves and agreeing to experi-ences that diminish their self-worth...just for the sake of having a man in their lives. I've watched them ignore their inner gangster when they've needed it most, and I've also observed them lacking vulnerability at crucial moments in their relationships because they are, to be frank, scared to death of both scenarios. So, I beg of you, take a break from snapping selfies and texting to pay attention. I'm here to help you love dating again and to share some knowledge enchanting women possess. Yes, my love, YOU are enchanting.

Believe it!!! You're a woman, so being enchanting comes with the territory. I don't care what you look like, how you dress, or what you believe. And, if your best friend tells you otherwise, get rid of her. Now. She's lying to you.

I know you aren't going to just take me at my word—which is also something you should *never* do with men—so let me share a bit more about myself so that you aren't trusting me blindly. Because I know that lots of people in this world feel as though education, money, and power give one authority (If you don't, then good for you.), I'm going to begin with the following information: I have a doctorate; I see actual patients...lots of them; and I own a multi-million-dollar business. However, oddly, I am also a woman who put being a doctor on hold to get a master's degree in art. So, before Katie convinced me to write this book I was, among other things, an art writer.

I have two homes, two cars, and a couple of really great closets. I've traveled the world. I LOVE fashion and art. *Yes, doll, I'm boujee,* BUT, if you're one of those Katies who gets all judge-y and excited by that last statement, then let me reassure you that I'm a small-town girl at heart. I was raised at the end of a gravel road, by two people who came from very little, in a town with a population of less than 500. While growing up, I road ATVs, ran around farms, and jumped into pick-up trucks. In my current life, you're as likely to find me in old cut-offs as you are in designer clothes and my Porsche.

I now live on an island, but I've called major metropolitan cities, including New York, home for most of my life. I am undefined and unpredictable. I bet you feel that way too because, duh, you're female. So, for all intents and purposes, I don't think it's much of a stretch to say that, when it comes to being female, I'm pretty much as free as one can get. No one tells me what to do. I call my own shots. I do whatever my little heart desires. I hire expensive attorneys to deal with my shit. I travel wherever I want to go. I stay in five-star hotels. I fuck and date whomever I please.

For those of you Katies who need experience as proof that I'm worthy of your time, let me also share this: I was married to a man many women would consider a dream guy. He was a "big man on campus", became a high-powered attorney, and looked a bit like Matthew McConaughey when we were together. I left him for my Greek lover who was also a doctor and a giant pain in the ass. *I know, I know!! Cheaters never win, which is the reason I never did **that** again.* Since then, I've had the beautiful and complicated pleasure of dating, loving, and hating a countless number of men. Most of the guys I spend time with now aren't doctors or lawyers. Do I care what they do for work? Not really. I'm much more concerned with how they treat me and who they are emotionally. I would encourage you to get to a place where you can prioritize the latter as well.

Honestly, the number of men I have known and attracted has always left me a bit perplexed. Someone once told me I just speak their language. Others have said I have a "je ne sais quoi". But, for the most part, I've never been able to put my finger on the exact reason so many men have come into my life, whether it be to torture me, bless me, amp up my sex life, serve as a muse, or force me to take a hard look in the mirror.

Do you know those women who constantly complain that they never meet guys? Aliens. I don't understand these chicks at all because I *always* meet men. I would encourage you to find a way to do the same. My own experience and personal growth have proven to me, and continue to validate my opinion, that we evolve by intensely engaging with the world. And one of the ways we do that is by participating in romantic relationships and dating.

In this book, I'm going to be tossing you little nuggets of wisdom that I have gained through my interactions with—you guessed it—men. I can tell you that some of my advice can also be applied in business, if you so choose. Let me tell you, I've dealt with some shitty motherfuckers in business, and I handle these men in *much* the same way I do the ones that I date.

Despite this being written from a woman's perspective based on dating men, I hope that anyone can scoop up this book and draw some understanding about romantic relationships, especially because, in most every workable couple, one person has a more dominant masculine or feminine energy. Even though I have had sexual encounters with women and have also been interested in a few of them romantically, I don't feel that I've had enough experience with the dynamics that occur in same-sex dating to create adequate threads for this book, so please accept my apologies if it seems overly conventional. Remember, I wrote this for Katie and for all the other Katies out there who sincerely desire a healthy dating life or even a long-term commitment with a male. When I'm speaking about men in this book, I am talking about those who gravitate to and prefer to date women.

Of course, because I'm writing a book about dating men, I'm going to be sharing some commonalities that I have seen within a particular subset of the population, but you need to know there are *always* exceptions. Take what I'm saying and put my theories to the test when you are dating. Always, always, always, circle back to your own intuition and develop it enough so that you can trust in what your body and mind are telling you. For example, I'm going to be telling you that "Men are cockroaches." To this day, I have only met one man who left never to return. I was shaken by this experience, but I have dated enough men to be confident about making the statement that "Men are cockroaches." I'll tell you what I mean later, but conclusions drawn by me are tendencies I have observed and not absolutes. I'm not a fucking scientist.

I realize that when I call myself a feminist and write about conventional dating that there are going to be women who feel annoyed. "We don't need men!" "This chick is setting us up for gender roles! How dare she?!" Goodness. Take it or leave it, but I'm actually not a woman who thinks men and women are the same. They aren't. *By their very definition, masculine and feminine energy—and even the biology of men and women—are not the same.* Please, FOR THE LOVE OF GOD, stop pretending men and women are the same. We are *not* the same. Never will be. I'm writing this from *my* perspective, so calm the fuck down if you think what I'm sharing is reductive. Or, instead, I would highly encourage you to sit down and write your own book, which isn't as easy as it looks.

Ladies, we don't need to hate men to know that we deserve to have the same *rights and level of respect* that they do, but there is a difference in the statement I just made versus saying "We are the same as men." Thank you to all the women who fought for our rights in the workplace and for making sure we can vote, but some of you have gone overboard. If you don't think within every balanced relationship there exists specific roles people play, then you are dead wrong. If you want to live your life on your own because you genuinely love your independence and freedom and sincerely don't enjoy male energy, then get on with your bad self, sister. But sending men messages that we no longer need them has left many of them passive, let down, and confused. Those same messages have also put women in the position of managing much more than they should inside of their romantic partnerships (if you want to call them that) and has left them drained and frustrated.

These women are making the money. They are taking care of the kids. They are paying someone to work on their homes. And what are their men doing besides occasionally fucking them? Nothing. These men haven't even learned to provide emotional support for their partners—which is a great way to balance the masculine energy that many women bring to their relationships—because, um, "Women can do it all." Look, we can absolutely do it all, but do you *really* want to?! I feel we deserve love, sex, nurturing, empathy, and support inside of our romantic relationships, if we choose to have them, just like we deserve equal pay. To receive those things, you have to be able to stand on your own two feet first, and this is where feminists got it right. If you can't, then you will never be able to walk away from a one-sided relationship. You will also never have the kind of romantic partnership we all deserve.

Why, Katie?

I think it's really important that we establish why men are worth loving and also why I'm encouraging you to go through the frustration of dating and occasionally dealing with bad guys. You might need to be reminded of the reason you continue to engage with men other than wanting to get "married" or to "settle down". Do you *really* want to be settled or down? I want my life to be full of passion and adventure. For me, marriage was once a part of having passion and adventure in my life. In this moment, it isn't. If you don't shift your focus from meeting a goal to, instead, enjoying every itty-bitty moment of dating and what it means to have the attention of a man and to feel alive, then you're missing out on the entire point; not to mention the potential you have of growing through—and because of—these beautiful, challenging creatures. Plus, as a feminist who believes in love and equality, I'm tired of all the male-bashing. I actually have a strong theory that God is a woman, and she was smart enough to know that we need men, just not in the way you may think.

So, why do we love men? Let me count the ways...except there aren't enough. But let's name a few anyway, shall we? We love the way they smell, smile, send flowers, build and lift things that we often can't, offer to pay for dinner—even when they can't afford it—just to impress us, text us "good morning", tell us how pretty we are without our make-up, and get-off on seeing us get-off. They take us places we would never have seen otherwise. They do things with us that they absolutely hate doing just to make us happy. Afterwards, they *thank us* for just showing up. Women don't do that, men do. Come on, ladies, give them some credit...*that's awesome.*

Men have also, inadvertently, helped us to examine ourselves through many of their attempts to control us and to convince us that we are less than magnificent. Some of them have left us abandoned. Knowing them for real—instead of the "fairy-tale" version of them—has made us grow-up and, also, forced us to dig deep. They've pushed us, unknowingly, to fight. They've made us seek self-awareness, break patterns, and find ways to be more self-sufficient and less co-dependent. Aren't we truly badass forces of nature, in large part, because of them? I think so.

You are Unique

Now, use your beautiful brains and always remember that you are your own person. Even though I've been told I have some valuable dating wisdom to share, I am not you. Recognizing our individuality is a key factor in being desirable and also in creating our most ideal lives and scenarios. You are YOU. Dating *requires* intuition and creativity. Enhancing these skills is a must, because, if you don't, you're going to be treating every man like a clone of the one before. Society, and especially other single women who are frustrated, have a way of trying to convince us that all men, and women, are exactly the same. To buy into this theory and operate from this belief is a big mistake in dating. Intuition is a magical, a.k.a. witchy, skill that every woman possesses.

I strongly believe that, unless a man has a very strong feminine energy—and I have known a few—intuition and sensitivity are distinct advantages women have over men. Generally, men were given stronger frames so that they could kick the shit out of people, which is why we created the police and laws. We were given the gift of intuition, which is why our female ancestors were burned at the stake. So, what I'm saying here is to get the whole "rules" concept out of your head with regards to dating men. HOWEVER, there are definitely some rules you should live by and those rules should be created by, and for, *you*. I know I have a few of my own so that I can maintain integrity with myself. And, to me, that's how we know who we are.

For instance, I am *not* a cheater. If I say I'm committed to someone then, damnit, I am. Why? Because, as I already shared with you, once I cheated on someone. I still feel it was one of the most disrespectful actions I have ever taken in my life. And, also, because I have been cheated *on*, I am well aware of how terrible it feels to be manipulated and lied to. Additionally, I am a person who makes an effort to live by my word. If the other person wants to lie and cheat, let them.

As much as we'd like to, we just can't control what other people do. I like to preserve my own karma and walk away from relationships knowing that I did the best that I could. So, the point is, this is just one example of *me* and part of my unique code. Know what your own rules are and live by them. This might even mean you being, and stating, that you are polyamorous. Respect other people and be honest with them. Make sure your love interest respects your core values as well, because, if they don't, then they need to move on and so do you.

You being YOU also means taking what God, the universe, quantum physics, or whatever you believe in, gave you and working it. Let me tell you what I "work" just to give you an idea: I work my style. I work my sass. I work my intelligence. I also work my sensual, sexual nature—not to be confused with being easy because, ladies, that I am *not*.

Let me also give you some examples of what I *do not* work: I don't work my giant ass. I don't have one. I don't work my light-as-a-feather, go-with-the-flow attitude. I stay in my own flow and welcome others to come into it. I don't work my ability to cook because I order take-out every day. Take what you have, your greatest assets—which might actually *be* your giant ass, whimsical personality, or ability to make a mean crème brûlée —and work that shit until it can be worked no more. You will attract men, and all people for that matter, who love *you* for *you*. I used to have this friend—note the past tense—who would always say: "Men are *all* into curves." She was always saying the word "all". *Really?* Did her brain fall out of her ear while I wasn't looking? I beg to differ. Prince William chose Kate Middleton for fuck sake. He didn't choose Pamela Anderson—she was for Tommy Lee, at least briefly. I love my teeny-weeny chest and I've had men tell me the same. I can knock a man's socks off with my eyes alone. Get a grip. And, if you have a friend like the one I just mentioned, then tell her to open her mind.

I think that most of us, in theory, understand that being authentic and embracing everything about ourselves is vital in life and in dating. Sure, there is compromise, but then there is *compromise*. Don't try to fit the mold, or pretend to be someone you aren't, for anyone. Why not? Because, eventually, playing pretend is going to come back and bite you in the ass. You're going to want what you want whether you hook that man in the beginning or not. And you're also going to stop pretending to be a cook, if you aren't and you hate it, at some point. When that moment comes, your relationship—maybe one you gave lots of time to—will start falling apart. You'll begin to resent HIM for not making YOU dinner. He'll feel angry that you stopped being the girl he thought you were, and then, *boom*, you're back to dating after wasting precious time on someone who made no sense for you. We don't have endless amounts of time here on earth. Let's not waste it on men who make no sense for us.

I realize that being genuine and emotionally open with the opposite sex can be scary and sometimes challenging, but the more honest you are, the better. Living in truth will result in you attracting your tribe, and, lovely, the man you want is part of that tribe.

Now, before you start going out and strutting your stuff, let's get clear on who you are *not*. I don't want you to misinterpret the above and start thinking that whatever bullshit garbage you throw at a man is "you".

Many women are confused about who they think they are because they haven't come to know who they really are. Some of them are trying to be like their friends or emulate celebrities. Others are still attempting to be who their parents and families have told them to be. You have to shake any and all identities that are not really you. Sure, as women we all wear different hats, but those hats *all* need to fit. Do the work. Be brave enough to walk into your own darkness. A lot of spiritual people call this "shadow work". I'm not going to elaborate on this here but if you haven't explored your own shadow, then I would highly encourage you to hop to it. Your most powerful and attractive self usually comes from a part of you that you've been encouraged to hide. So, what often happens in dating, is that you will attract someone on the surface who seems right for you but isn't.

A great example of this is what happened to me in my marriage, which occurred for me at the ripe old age of twenty-two. Let me tell you, my ex-husband was pretty close to perfect, but he wasn't perfect for me. Back then, I still thought I was someone I wasn't. I didn't understand why our marriage made me feel unhappy. And the reason that it did was because he was, and I think he still is, conventional and pragmatic. I wasn't yet my artsy, wild self. I hadn't discovered my own creativity. I had been valedictorian, voted most likely to succeed, and was a pageant girl. *Sidenote: nothing wrong with that, I killed every interview I had to go through to become successful because of those crazy pageants.* I had done everything perfectly and, damnit, I was also going to marry the perfect guy.

Fast forward. Now, I have a few tattoos. I have a style that is my own. I'm a bit flamboyant. I'm sweet but, trust me, I will cut you when pushed. I go against the grain, but my younger self wouldn't dare. I didn't know who I was and I also didn't have a voice of my own. So, I ended up with someone who also followed the rules because that's who he was and is. My poor ex-husband dealt with me crying in the bathroom A LOT while neither of us understood why I was miserable. I felt trapped and alone. The reason I felt alone was because, even though I was married and with someone, I didn't have me. Eventually, my lover showed up and encouraged my sexuality and creativity—thank goodness—and that was the end of a romance-turned-marriage that lasted about six years longer than it should have. My ex is now married to a chick who is perfect for him. He has a child. We still e-mail on occasion. I don't have children; I don't want them. But you can bet that, if I would have stayed, I'd have a couple of them right now because he *really* wanted offspring. What a disaster that would have been!

Some women also haven't figured out how to manage all that they are. They have the ability to call on parts of themselves when required, but they are stuck thinking they are one piece of their complicated inner pie or the other. Let me use the "power girl" as an example...

To me, power girls are women who have worked their asses off and make their own money. This usually requires them calling on their masculine energy. Some of these women are cool with playing the same role in their relationships, which is the masculine role. For instance, I have a friend from graduate school who has a very strong core and work ethic. She and her husband have been together for years. She makes the money. He does a lot of work for their church and takes most of the responsibility for their kids: getting them to and from baseball practice, etc. He also cooks. You get the picture. Having a man who occupies a more feminine role in their relationship works for them. She wouldn't have it any other way and she loves and respects him for it.

But, a lot of power girls DO NOT want that. They want the alpha male. They want a man who takes charge and some even desire a guy who makes more money than them. They want to go home and escape their masculinity and fall into the feminine, but they haven't figured out how to do that, so they play the masculine role in dating. They believe, because they are so fucking forceful and powerful in other arenas of their lives, that they are going to fix and force a relationship. They also haven't figured out, because they have to be a motherfucker in their jobs, that the key to having that alpha male is to show their softer side and vulnerability. Don't get me wrong, I'm not encouraging passivity, but what I am encouraging is for you, whether you are a "power girl" or not, to get to know what it is that you want. If you have an extremely feminine woman living inside of you, stop offering to pay for dinners when you don't want to. Stop making plans for your man. Let him take the lead.

I also want to invite you to ask yourself if you have been real when communicating with men or if you have been communicating with them out of fear. *You **are not** your fears.* This is much trickier than most realize. I still catch myself acting out of fear because of events triggered from childhood wounds or maybe a trauma from something that happened in a prior relationship. Make sure, before you make crucial decisions about a relationship, that you are absolutely certain that your actions and words are in line with your healthy, aware self.

For instance, when a man goes silent is it *really* you who's reaching out to him because you want to talk? Or is fear dominating that choice? Fear often guides you to take action out of being scared of abandonment or rejection, so instead of holding your own and sticking to what you know when a boundary is crossed or when a man is completely out of line, you cave out of fear. Let me repeat: *Fear is not you.* Get to know the difference. Women who have relationships that are satisfying and long-term are very clear on this. These women also know not to force a relationship. They know that they are completely worthy of a man who shows up for them. They don't care how long it takes because their lives are awesome either way. They are also capable of admitting when they're wrong, but they don't do it because they might lose a guy. They are committed to maintaining their side of the street, and that takes guts.

There's a Type

Being a mystic and a romantic—quite naturally—has gotten me into trouble in dating. Like many women who live for the rush of falling in love, I have been the girl who has chosen romantic interests based on chemical attraction and the elevated beat of my heart. I've thrown caution to the wind, ignored red flags, and have followed "the signs". Having dealt with men in this manner has burned me in the past, big time. If I'm being completely honest, I still struggle with viewing a man from a logical point of view, but this book is for you and Katie and not about the weaknesses I still have, so let's turn my mistakes into an easy way for you to evaluate someone of the opposite sex that's beneficial for both you *and* them. You'll be saving everyone a lot of frustration.

Let's look at some tendencies, or categories, that the average man is likely to fall into. Again, men and women are different. One significant way they are different is that women tend to view life more broadly. They have a level of complexity to them that men just don't *generally* possess. In contrast, most men are likely to focus their energy in one, maybe two, directions. A woman's energy tends to be more dispersed. She will likely allow herself to be interested in a variety of subjects and her goals often translate into platforms that assist her in doing other things she's interested in.

For instance, when it comes to a career, most women don't just seek money; they secretly, or not so secretly, desire influence. Maybe the idea of money and power drove them to reach their goal but, usually, once they arrive, they use their positions to instill positive change and to inspire others. Sometimes they'll use their money and success to advance their passions the way I have.

Women have a natural curiosity about life that, even after they make a decision, will pull them into other directions. They are complex as fuck. This is also why women can multi-task and do about a zillion different things at once while men usually don't and can't. Women can be complicated and a complete mystery to men, a big reason why many of them find us fascinating and irresistible. What's the beauty of this, sometimes frustrating, difference we have with the male species? Our ability to characterize who they are is much easier for us than it is for them. Why? Because, unlike women, they tend to fall into categories. I know this may sound as though I'm dumbing men down but—and I say this out of complete respect for men—they are *usually* that simple if you let them be.

For simplicity's sake and to offer you a way to visualize this, let me provide a comparative metaphor linked to nature: Think of a woman as an octopus and a man as a fish. Both live in water, but an octopus changes color with its environment. It has beautiful arms that extend in all directions.

Being with a certain type of man brings with it advantages and disadvantages. I once fell in love with a guy who worked at a coffee shop and had a criminal record. Working at a coffee shop is perfectly fine and criminals often reform but, as I said, I'm a doctor with a successful business. Instead of just sleeping with him, which was my intention and also something I *don't* recommend because women emotionally bond with the men they sleep with whether they like it or not, I tried to create a relationship with him. Impossible. Our level of ambition, life goals, and general morality were not a match. Advantage: the sex was phenomenal and I felt worshipped by him. Disadvantage: he was an emotional adolescent and a mess. Use your brain in dating as much as you do your heart. You'll avoid a lot of unnecessary drama and pain.

I should warn you before we continue that most men will try to convince you that they do not fall into the neat little boxes I'm about to introduce. They love to use their *words* to paint a picture of the kind of man they think they are. Why? Because men are well aware that most women use their hearts to make their decisions. Goodness, these same men might even *believe* they are a different kind of man than they are because they want to be. *How sweet...doesn't matter.* Until proven otherwise, he is who he is. Men are the greatest of salesmen. We can't hold it against them, because they want to win us over, capture our hearts, and, above all, avoid missing out on us. But, don't allow your heart to move in until after you've watched and observed a man to the point that it's almost clinical. Use what I'm about to share as a starting point and assume what I am saying is correct about him until proven otherwise. Write down your observations and initially categorize him based on the principles below. Afterwards, validate or dismiss one or the other based on *his consistent actions and NOT his words.*

In my opinion, when it comes to men, there are three essential principles that you're going to want to keep in mind. The first is that **they fall on a curve from left-brained to right,** and the best way to evaluate whether they are one or the other is to look at their profession or their career path. Right-brains are your creatives and operate more cyclically. Left-brains are goal-oriented, linear thinkers. For instance, I was operating on left-brain mentality until I was about thirty, then I had a shift and started to explore the mystical, art, and writing. I am a person who fought to break free of a single-based identity, that of a doctor and left-brained professional, so that I could feel more whole. I was suppressing and repressing an essential part of who I am. This required me to learn (and, believe me, I'm still learning) how to slide in and out of right and left-brained thinking. This *is not* the norm for most men. The majority of them are usually much more one than the other.

Ask yourself what kind of man and life it is that you want. Some women want the house, dog, and 2.5 kids. They like stability and predictability. Those are girls who are best paired with left-brained men. Others need to feel free with their partner and inspired by them. They don't care if they own a home. They think kids will keep them from seeing the world. These women also bore easily. See where I'm going with this…?

For comparison, let's look at the difference between dating a financial guy and an artist. Can you think of two people who are, typically, more opposite? Usually, the financial guy is a workaholic animal. He's a logical thinker and needs a strong base. He can't wrap his head around the fact that you need to hear from him more than once a week and *why* you're not more understanding of his job, which is the most important thing on Earth to him. Any woman who's going to be by his side had better understand that or feel totally okay with having a lover. Now, on the other hand, the artist has a tendency to be more expressive and sensitive. Sometimes, he may also exhibit a stronger feminine side because his decisions are based more on feeling than logic. What's the catch? Financial guy can afford to stay in fancy hotels and eat at expensive restaurants. He's also going to want to be calling the shots. Artist guy may not be able to help you pay for groceries but he might pick a daisy for you on the way to your house. Additionally, he probably doesn't have a problem with you taking the lead.

The second essential principle is that **men have a temperature.** For instance, my ex-husband was about 20 degrees. My lover was 150. If you can't take the heat, then get out of the kitchen. I consider high-temperature men to be those who thrive on drama and who are intensely complicated and sexual. High-temperature guys are your bad boys and bad boys exist in every profession. Low-temperature men don't rock the boat as much but they are probably not going to give you multiple orgasms. High-temperature men get off on seeing you angry and out of sorts—*that's passion, baby.* They also have a difficult time with monogamy. Low-temperature men make choices that are often based on the avoidance of stirring up negative emotions—for either of you—and they tend to love the idea of being a partner. High temps create noise in your life; noise that often isn't audible. Low temps, well, they keep it chill. No, I am sorry to say, you are not getting all of the positive qualities that come with high temperature and low temperature individuals in one man. You're going to have to choose which you prefer but you can have it all...like by dating a low-temperature guy and owning a great vibrator.

The last principle is **age matters.** "What?!!!" you say. "Blasphemy!!!" I just heard from another. Sister, you can deny this all you want and, well, I know that you think you have all the wisdom in the world in your twenties, but, take it from me, you don't. Just like youth has the tendency to carry with it, well, less wrinkles and a tighter ass, and—in the case of a male—a much stronger libido and lots of fun, age usually brings maturity and wisdom. No, I am not the woman I was ten years ago. Thank goodness. I know much more now about life than I ever did before. I know more about who I am and what I want and, I suspect, my 56-year-old self will be much smarter than the one writing this book. So, put your big girl panties on and receive this hard-to-swallow pill of truth: *Age…fucking …matters.*

Let's face it. In contrast to their older counterparts, younger guys are hungry for life and for women. They are wild, unpredictable, and exciting. They tend to be more sexually driven and open to new experiences. Many of them maintain a curiosity about life and people. They haven't fully developed the same level of cynicism possessed by many older men because they haven't been around the block. They also have less baggage, like children and ex-wives. They can be refreshing and energetic.

Many women carry the false belief that a younger man will be more submissive. They think that being with a man who's much younger than they are will result in them having more control within the relationship. Wrong. Please don't trick yourself into thinking that you're going to tell a younger man what to do. The opposite is more likely. Conventional wisdom tells us that they are more moldable and that older men are stuck in their ways. Younger men are not more *moldable*. They are stubborn and ready to take on the world. They need more freedom inside of their romantic relationships than older men do. Also, most of them haven't suffered or failed, yet, which is a major component of growth and maturity. Yes, older men can be stuck in their ways...like in the way they prefer having their laundry folded, refuse to sleep on the left side of the bed, and have zero interest in trying your espresso martini. *They've been drinking whisky for twenty years, damnit, and they aren't changing now.*

Men get more stable, not to mention have a stronger base, the older they get. If they haven't, then you know something is amiss. Older men tend to have moved through their need to conquer—life, business, and women. They are more direct and self-assured...*what you see is usually what you get.* They've either made it or given up on an idealistic life and dreams that they knew were probably unrealistic in the first place. Unlike the younger man, they aren't run by ambition and competition. Either way, they are in a place of acceptance, for better or worse. All of this usually means that the older man, as long as he's single and available, has more space in his life for you. His friends are married. He doesn't want to be the last one standing. He understands the importance of having a woman by his side.

Let me tell you something else that I've learned by dating men of all ages—because I don't want women to leave convinced that I'm advocating for the older man. As a woman in her forties who has a tendency to attract younger men, I have seen another major distinction that currently exists in our culture but isn't necessarily being talked about.

Men who were raised by baby boomers are very different than men who are millennials. It's been my personal experience that millennials are much more comfortable with strong women than their Gen X counterparts. So, here is my theory: I believe that millennial men were exposed to women in their households, specifically their mothers, who probably carried more weight inside of their relationships than their older counterparts had. Their mothers were less likely to fall into gender roles and expected to "behave". These men were also growing up during a time when girls were being told they could do anything boys could. I find men who are ten years (sometimes more) younger than me completely comfortable with my success and independence and, I feel, this is because they have no reason to think otherwise.

I have dated several Gen-X men and it's my personal experience that they don't like being held accountable by the women in their lives and have a difficult time under-standing their own emotions, which are generally repressed, and yours. You'll probably experience a frustrating dynamic with them if you are a certain kind of woman, one where you feel judged and encouraged to not share your feelings and emotions openly. Their mothers didn't, and they certainly weren't pushed to share their own emotions either. *Real men don't do that*, in their minds. Your emotions and voice are often inconvenient for them. I can't tell you how many times I have been told by men my age and a bit older that I'm "too sensitive" when I express how I feel. The younger men I have met, millennials, are completely comfortable with being vulnerable and not downplaying emotions.

Know where you are in your life and what you are willing to tolerate, then understand and accept what you are most likely to get with men of a certain age.

Be 'Nice'

"What Are Little Boys Made of?"

What are little boys made of?
What are little boys made of?
Snips and snails
And puppy-dogs' tails,
That's what little boys are made of.

What are little girls made of?
What are little girls made of?
Sugar and spice
And everything nice,
That's what little girls are made of.

—Author, unknown patriarchal asshole

Wow. Don't we all feel just a bit sick, and maybe even angry, after reading that nursery rhyme, one that's been recited to children for over 200 years? And *why* does it feel triggering? Because, there it is, right there in black and white: Girls are sweet as sugar and boys get to have all the fun. However, the secret poison in that charmingly sweet ditty is a nasty word, still snaking through our culture, biting the necks of little girls everywhere: "nice".

I have a feeling—at least I hope I'm right in assuming—that most women now would think twice about passing along damaging, even dangerous, stereotypes that assist a patriarchal society designed by men for men, which is no longer working for anyone, including men. And, in my humble yet passionate opinion, I strongly feel that there isn't a more pervasive word in the English language that has been put upon women than "nice". Actually, as I keep writing the word "nice", I just become more and more angry. Call me anything. Call me a "bitch". *Yes...thank you very much...occasionally, I am.* Call me a "motherfucker". *Oh, you had better believe I've got a baby motherfucker living inside of me. You DO NOT want to know her.* Call me a crazy cunt who is out of control and can never be helped. *Hmmm. Probably.* But, you had better take a large

sideways step if you tell me to "be nice".
Fuck you.

Some of you might think I'm over-reacting by giving so much power to this word. But, before you jump to conclusions, I'd like you to think about all the rapes, sexual harassment, and incest that may have been avoided if girls would have been raised—and if women had been encouraged—to stand up for themselves, make a fuss, and to tell the truth no matter what the cost, if they hadn't been pushed to be nice instead. If you're just nice, you'll remain safe and protected, right? *WRONG.*

Women like to blame men for a lot of terrible things that have happened to them, and I have definitely been one of those women. But, we can't just look at the actions of power-hungry, deranged men while we are attempting to create a safe and empowering world for ourselves and our daughters. Women, probably as much or more than men, have been *creating environments* for abusive and disrespectful men to thrive in and we continue to do so. We have a responsibility as women to stop this. We owe it to ourselves and to the women who come after us. We *have* to drop "playing nice" in every facet of our lives for there to be a shift away from the expectation of being "good" and move into the reality of women being flawed and human. You know, the same reality we have been allowing men for thousands of years. Even Jesus got to toss over a table and lose his temper. I've never heard anyone call him crazy.

Do you know who told me to be "nice" the most when I was growing up? My mother. On the contrary, my father didn't care if I was nice and never told me to be—not once. He told me I could do and become anything I wanted. Sure, he had plenty of faults, but concerning himself with how others felt about his daughter wasn't one of them. That's a real mind-fuck, huh? Except that it isn't because, the truth is, even though men still have difficulty controlling their animal urges with women, they aren't the ones telling us to be nice. Women are.

Like the majority of women on this planet, I have been a victim of abuse, discrimination, and harassment over the course of my existence. But, ladies, I am here to tell you that nothing has screwed with my life as much as all the times my mother told me to be or act nice, when she could have, and should have, encouraged me to be my naturally strong and powerful self. Her words have acted as a catalyst for many of the bad decisions I have made, and still occasionally make, with the following: business, male colleagues, female employees, friends, and romantic relationships. The story I was told, and it's the same one many of you were sold, is this: "Be nice or people will reject and abandon you. Be nice or no one will like you. If you aren't nice, you will have nothing and nobody." And, if you were like me, before you hit adolescence, you were taught that keeping your mouth shut, despite it being repressive and eating away at your soul like a cancer, would hold your family and life together.

My mother needed me to be nice to protect the image of her own life. Over time, and maybe even due to the insistence of her own mother, she had become convinced that she had to be seen as perfect by the outside world. She held on to an impossible standard set up for her by women and attempted to do the same for her daughter. To her credit, she probably did this because she thought it would keep her daughter and her family safe. Well, it didn't and it doesn't.

Being nice comes with a price: the loss of integrity, dignity, self-respect, and self-esteem. And forcing yourself into being nice for the sake of having a romantic relationship, at the cost of losing your core being, has *major* consequences like anxiety, depression, escapism mentality, addiction, and, sometimes, loss of life itself because, for some women, death is more appealing than facing being seen.

I think it's important to dissect just a few of the external pressures/illusive treasures that could get you hooked into thinking that you need to be the nice girl to survive, or those that can trap you in scenarios where you feel there is no alternative to playing the nice girl. Falling into the nice girl myth usually comes from attachments to an external reality and validation from said reality. Before I go on, it's important to note—and for you to *never* forget—that anything that exists outside of you has *zero* permanence and can disappear or change at a moment's notice. We have very little control in our lives other than the control we have over ourselves. You might change and move in all kinds of different directions over the course of your journey but, everywhere you go, there you are…until death do you part. Why am I going off on a Buddhist tangent? Because understanding this principle moves us from fear into love. In turn, we gain everything including power over ourselves. We also drop the nice girl we thought was us.

First: **jobs and money**. Darling, jobs are everywhere. Money comes and goes. Hell, the company you treasure—especially with technology and the global market shifting by the minute—could go out of business any day. Retail businesses are closing, taxi companies are becoming obsolete, and even the number of teachers and professors is diminishing due to the growing number of online courses. So, a strong possibility exists that the coveted professional position you hold may not even *exist* in another five years, *but* any psychological damage you could suffer by being the nice girl and keeping your mouth shut by letting someone grope or abuse you, will remain for a lifetime. Unfortunately, but to my point, while I was editing this book, but long after I wrote what you just read, a pandemic hit. Don't make me tell you that I'm right.

Second: **your man**. The last time I checked, there were men with lovely penises walking about everywhere. To be exact, there are almost 4 billion penises in the world. That's a lot of penises. And many of those penises are attached to grown men who want actual relationships! Some of them are even frustrated with the bullshit garbage, weird manipulative games that inauthentic women are still playing. Isn't it *possible* that the partner for you is out there just waiting while you're holding on to a man who couldn't possibly level up to the force of nature you truly are? I'm going to really frighten you...you might even find that you *don't want* a man. Maybe what you want instead is freedom or the company of women, but no one ever gave you permission to think any of that was acceptable. Those of us who read *Eat, Pray, Love* were inspired by Elizabeth Gilbert's quest, right? She jumped off a cliff, found herself, and, as a just reward, also ended up with the love of her life and the man of her dreams. So romantic and perfect. Newsflash: Years later, she left that man and ended up with a woman.

Third: **your children**. "But what about my children?? They need their father!" Of course they are better off with two balanced human beings who love and cherish them remaining in their lives! The more love and goodness the better, I say. But they *don't* need you to expose them to an unhealthy relationship they will almost certainly mirror. What's *usually* at the heart of two people with children staying together "for the sake of the children" isn't the kids at all; it's the fear of the unknown, being seen as a failure, and releasing a relationship based on co-dependency. I have been treating children for nearly twenty years. I've also been treating adults for the same amount of time. Which group do you think is the most resilient? The answer to that question is not the adults. So, what are you protecting them from? The world is chaotic, unpredictable, and messy. They know it, and they don't need you selling them perfect little stories of the people they can't be and a world that doesn't exist. They *need* truth. Before they got to know you—and consequentially received your conditioning—they lived in truth, as children do. Don't use your kids, or any relationship you have with a family member, as an excuse not to grow.

The false notion of the nice girl has pushed women into tolerating almost anything men subject us to for the sake of obtaining and keeping a romantic relationship. Some of us don't even know we're being mistreated, objectified, undermined, and disrespected because we've become so immune. Especially if we are over a certain age, some of us become so afraid of being alone that we will accept scenarios with men that we wouldn't have dared lived with in our twenties. So, we play nice, and the reason we play nice is because we have attachments. Drop your attachments, especially the one you may have to a specific man or the thought that you need a relationship. You don't *need* a relationship to be happy...but...you might *prefer* to have one.

The Non-Nice Girl

So, what are some qualities of the non-nice girl, and how does she handle herself? "If I'm not 'nice' then how can I keep a man around?" The real question is this: *How can you train yourself to keep you around?* If you are doing the opposite and making choices on how to keep someone in your life then, again, you are living in fear and that fear is based on the need to control and attach to an outcome or, even worse, the other person. People who love you truly love you as, and for, you. Period.

First things first. Let's clarify how the nice girl handles herself in situations with men and how being the non-nice girl is *not* about being unkind to others. Remember, this book is about you being authentic and, often, your authentic self is kind!! The nice girl isn't kind. She's nice. She's nice when she's hurt. She's nice when she's pissed. She gets on a sailboat with her man when she knows she's going to end up vomiting over the side because she suffers from motion sickness. Basically, the nice girl is a woman who abuses herself into submission because she doesn't know how to use her voice. Her nice-ness translates into her being unkind, to herself. The non-nice girl says to her fisherman or boat-loving lover: "Sugar-pie, have fun. I'm not going to be on that boat because, as you know, I'll end up puking my guts up. Call me later." Can we all agree that if your man pushes you beyond that, doesn't give a shit about you being sick, because he wants to see you on that boat come hell or high-water, then he probably isn't a person you should be spending time with? Yes, let's all agree. People who love us don't want us to hurt ourselves, compromise our integrity, or end up vomiting.

I hope you can also see that communicating as the non-nice girl does not mean having to be hateful, bossy, or masculine. The non-nice girl has class. She knows how to use her words. She doesn't need to scream or throw things because she's not a child; she's a woman with power. Powerful women find creative ways to express how they feel without shaming or blaming and then they leave it up to the people they communicate with to respond. They use their words and actions to take care of themselves and to gain information about the other person and the relationship. They don't use either to manipulate or hurt men. They understand that if their fisherman boyfriend needs a girl on a boat, then it's okay if he finds one. *Plenty of fish in the sea.*

Non-nice girls cause a fuss and creating a fuss can often mean holding people to their word. When a man tells you he wants you to meet his mother and then sleeps with you and doesn't text—meaning push the buttons on his phone for a total of ten seconds for three solid weeks until he's bored—you're supposed to be *nice*? You had better not be.

Look, I know that it's uncomfortable to be direct and to say what you feel. But nothing worth having comes easy. Think about anything you value in your life. Didn't it require you to stretch yourself and to get out of your comfort zone? Relationships with others are no different. We owe it to each other to be honest and part of being honest is holding people accountable when they lie to, purposely trick, or hurt us. When we do this, is it about hooking a man? No, it isn't. Using your voice—or even ceasing communication, temporarily or permanently—to set things straight is about you empowering the person you know yourself to be and, if it's early in your connection, it's also about establishing boundaries and dynamics.

Even though we aren't, for the sake of this book, attempting to help the other person grow, we actually are by taking these kinds of actions. When others observe you living in integrity, bravery, and self-respect, it gives them permission to do the same. Often, it inspires them to up-level. Goodness, you may be the only woman in the world a man has ever encountered who holds her own and who lives in authenticity. This often results in a man questioning behaviors he had never considered before in many arenas of his life, including dating. But, I think it's worth noting, that sometimes the other person's growth isn't the result of us communicating our needs in a real and grounded way because they aren't ready to grow. Maybe they don't want to change and are totally comfortable where they are. Shouldn't you respect their choice? How is trying to force a relationship and behaviors onto a man any different than someone violating your body? You don't want to be pushed into scenarios that are wrong for you, right?! Don't push him to be someone he isn't just so you can have a boyfriend.

Loving yourself and walking around with your head held high isn't optional. And, since this book is about dating, guess what else is going to happen? You will shift your frequency to match and attract a strong, no-nonsense king of a man. The universe has to comply. It's the law.

Frequency

Ooh-la-la, let's talk about one of my favorite subjects: frequency. *Fuck, I love this word.* Why? Because frequency is everything. As a mystical, high-vibe witch, I can tell you that the energy you possess, the way you feel, and the people you surround yourself with are all part of your frequency. They are playing a part in everything you create, consciously or not. And, unfortunately, most of it is unconscious, so, yeah, this is an important principle, one not to be dismissed, if you want a dreamy life.

Recently, I was playing back a reading I did for myself through tarot and this card was dynamite. The reading lead into the influence people have on one another. We influence those around us. And, in turn, they influence us. Everything you choose, all the actions you take, are drawing you closer to more of that stuff, whether it's icky or bananas. Want proof? The moment I started writing this book—*about dating*—an employee of mine approached me introducing me to a friend of hers. This male friend had published a book on romance. My employee had no idea I was writing a book on dating. She didn't even know I was writing at the moment. "What the fuck?!! That's crazy!" No, it isn't. The frequency you put yourself on through your actions and general vibe are creating your experience. No, you cannot just sit in your room thinking about owning a yacht and expect Amazon Prime to deliver. If fantasy thinking worked then Lenny Kravitz and I would have been walking down the aisle years ago. Also, *Lenny, if you're reading this, call me.*

You are in a dance with your life. You are in more of a relationship with the projected hologram that is your external world than you are with your man! And this relationship is reflective of the one you have with yourself. You are watching and feeling YOU. And you are responsible for designing the nightclub or movie that is your life. But wait, of course it's not that simple. Other people are here with us designing as well, right? So, your internal will and energy had better be stronger than what's out there. The Collective has an energy and that energy is STRONG. So, you need to make a choice. Is your nightclub going to be filled with the music and flowers you prefer? Are your best friends going to be there? Is the hot lover whom you know you want—and can literally feel inside of your bones—going to show up? Or, is your club going to have people in it who drain your energy while the DJ plays songs you can't dance to?

Yes, you are doing the salsa with your external experience. The statements I just made aren't empty spiritual love and light sentences meant to inspire you. They are the reality of the unseen world we live in. Ladies, I'm here to tell you, my life is on a super-high frequency, and I believe the reason is this: *I have learned to will and choose my own experience.* Sincerely, I walk around just knowing what's coming to me. My life has a fearlessness involved in it. Sure, most people are fearless about some of the choices they make but can you be fearless enough to say, "No, not good enough, Mr. External World. I'll wait?" You see, most people are so impatient that they will never see what's on the other side of being committed to high frequency. They say to themselves, "Ohhhh myyyy godddd, it's a sign! Here we go…" OF COURSE, your shift is going to bring sugar-laden signs, BUT, can you wait until that sign morphs into the person, job, or place you just *know* is exactly right for you? Most people cannot, because their fear, not what they dream of, is driving the bus that is their life. They are afraid of missing the window of having a baby. They would rather get married at twenty-five to a man who will never be a match than be alone…forever.

Sugar, if you don't want to be alone, just walk outside. I can promise you that there is a man who will give you the terrible pleasure of screwing you if given the chance. But, you, my dear goddess, are NOT going to follow an itty-bitty sign, which is usually created by your subconscious anyway (and your subconscious has a lot of junk and cobwebs that you probably don't want expressed in your external experience). Instead, you are going to *consciously* woman-up to create and have all the goods to go with it because you're reading this fucking book.

So, if you choose to continue seeing, or having sex with (yikes!), a guy who has no value for you, then what and who do you think you'll get more of? Take a moment. You're about to have an epiphany because I'm going to tell you why you are getting a bunch of trash you don't want and why you start to feel as though all guys are the same.

Once you choose, exchange energy with, or vibrate with another person, it usually takes at least THREE people or encounters, for that energy to die out and for your external world to reflect your new desires. Sorry, energy re-arranging isn't instant. I know, I know, I hate it too because, despite what I just shared, I am as impatient as fuck. Just prepare yourself and don't get discouraged when you run into the same problems with the next guy as the one before. Dismiss it and know your shift is coming. You have to be strong and ride it out.

Now you understand why your best girlfriend keeps connecting with the abuser or, in my case, why, for a while, I kept meeting attorneys, then New Yorkers no matter where I traveled (even Italy), then Jamaicans, and—wait for it—narcissists. If you are a high-level manifester who is living a non-linear life from the heart, then this is going to be your playbook.

What the fuck is a non-linear life from the heart? It's a life that requires sensitivity and massive awareness of knowing when to forge ahead and when to rest; it's one centered around connecting with your own feelings and not ignoring them. A non-linear life requires that you take those feelings and use them to inform your next course of action. A woman who lives a non-linear life from the heart is *free*. She watches, listens, and moves. She loves but isn't beholden to other people. She's onboard for magic and the experience. She knows she is in control of her life and that the illusions that the masses tell her exist are actually complete crap. She recognizes that she is influenced by everything, including but not limited to, the planets, her posse, the place where she chooses to reside—because every place on Earth has an energy—and her cycle. When you get in line with all of this and listen to the greatest gift you possess, your intuition, then you attract and manifest practically instantaneously. Like, tomorrow. It's scary. You are seriously that powerful.

Part of shifting into a high-frequency, up-leveled life is being able to let go of and ditch old energy that is no longer you. Now, I'm not saying that you have to do this, but *I'm telling you*, taking actions to get rid of old stuff will move you into the movie you want to be starring in—*faster*. And, faster, is what we always want. As I said, we don't have time to fuck around.

I'm constantly keying into the little secrets that life holds. I observe what's going on—the cause and effect of my life and actions—like a nuclear physicist. I study myself. I study my life. I'm a student of the unseen world and I suggest that you become one too. I'm not so sure that all the rules apply the same to all of us. I'm more convinced that we move up a ladder. Some people call this enlightenment. Whatever, I don't. I call it the school of life. Maybe you excelled in the first grade but that doesn't mean that you're going to be making the grades in college. And you can be smart as fuck but that doesn't necessarily result in you getting into graduate school. *Keep telling me how smart you are, and how you could have done this or that—but didn't—while I roll my eyes.* For most of us, what is required for us to enter graduate school?

First, we have to have the dream of getting into graduate school. Then, we have to be smart AND study AND work. We have to drag our asses out of bed and go to class. We also have to brave enough not to attempt to get a degree in mathematics when we are told by everyone we know how great we are at math, and how much money we could make if we just got a master's degree in math, when we know in our hearts that we play the piano better than Beethoven and couldn't give a shit about numbers.

If you want to stay in the first grade taking lunchtime naps and using crayons, go right ahead. Many people love this simplicity...feels easy and uncomplicated. Bitch, give me complicated. Give me every fucking experience I can possibly have while I can still get around because I signed up for *life*. I'm here to dig in. I'm here to find a way I can have everything my little heart desires and one of the ways I have done that is by getting rid of, or distancing myself from, people and things that made sense for the first-grader me but not the college me.

I started understanding this concept when, one year, as my single New Year's resolution, which I usually refuse to set, I created one goal: to up-level. I had made a decision that every part of my life was going to be better. And, holy shit, did it ever. The train on this got moving so fast that by the end of the year I was wiped out, but I had asked for it and it was awesome. My up-level began with a friend of mine convincing me to sell some of my clothes online. I started doing this and couldn't believe how good it made me feel. I got addicted to purging. I replaced my old stuff with the money I made. It began with me getting rid of jewelry and most of my wardrobe. I swear to you I had shit in my closet that I hadn't worn in ten years. I replaced it with more grown-up things that reflected how I wanted to look and feel. I was still driving my good ol' Mini Cooper with 90,000 miles along with my Jeep. Got rid of that and bought a Porsche. *Bless.* This effect snowballed. The apartment that I had owned for fourteen years went under contract and sold in record time. My business started hitting baller numbers that I had never reached before. Friends that made me feel like shit—most of whom cared A LOT more about themselves than they did me—and drained me? Gone. Friendships with those who were giving, reciprocal, and sensitive gained traction. I know you know what's coming next...the trashy, superficial men I loved to keep around? They disappeared too and men who were ambitious, deep, and creative started showing up.

Letting go isn't easy, especially if some of the people in our lives have been there for years. But, ask yourself, do they belong in the life you no longer want? Send them love and move along if that's the case. Purge, purge, purge...if you want a shift.

Sex

Ladies I'm not going to tell you who to sleep with and who not to, but we need to talk about sex. Do you realize the energetic exchange that occurs with sex? And, because you are female, you are the receptacle and the receiver of that energy. This means that the nastiness or amazingness of the person you just slept with, and his partners too, just got sent to you. *Holy shit.*

Let me share a really scary story with you to prove my point…

For a bit, I was sleeping with an artist who was absolutely magnificent in bed. I actually called his penis the Eiffel Tower, and, well, I don't think I need to explain this metaphor. Our sex was delicious. His energy sucked. Over time, I came to realize that he was legit bi-polar, and I'm not talking about the way every man in the universe claims his ex was bi-polar after their relationship ended because he realized she wasn't Mary Magdalene. This guy was in an institution as a kid, had been diagnosed as bi-polar, and refused to take his meds. Despite the roller-coaster, extreme nature of his personality, and one that was the closest thing to evil I have ever seen when he was on a low, I continued to see him. I loved his creative nature. He was hot. He was also sweet when he wasn't being awful.

Furthermore, as you have probably already guessed, I was totally addicted to our sex, so I ignored his shitty energy and grey aura, which he carried no matter his mood, for three solid months. Well, guess what? I got a yeast infection. But not just any yeast infection. One that lasted half a year. I was depressed. I was scared that I would never have sex again. Nothing I did made it go away. Until one day, a nurse told me how emotional energy can make our bodies do wacky stuff, and it suddenly occurred to me that I had hated myself for sleeping with someone who was terrible to me 50% of the time. That day I cried, like wept, for myself. It went away the next week. *I mean, fuck.*

Please, take it from your soul sister when I tell you to monitor who you have sex with and to pay attention to how that person makes you feel before you allow them to physically enter you. I realize many women and feminists tell us to act like men and do whatever we want, but just like any information that gets shared with you, it needs questioned. As I said, we are not men. And, yes, we have earned the right to choose and to have freedom, but that does not give us a free pass to ignore the consequences of our actions and how they might hurt us. With freedom comes responsibility.

The responsibility that comes with sexual freedom has been ignored by much of the male population for centuries. One of the reasons for this is because they don't experience the aftermath of sex and its resultant energetic impact the way we do. Again, while men are giving energy and leaving a trail, our bodies are stuck with receiving it: physically, mentally, and spiritually. Ever wonder why men usually seem less attached after sex, but women, generally, get more attached? Now you have a viable explanation (other than hormones and women, in theory, being more emotional than men) as to why this occurs.

And maybe you're a chick, like myself, who literally hears the person's thoughts and feels their feelings, whether it be depression or joy, after a sexual energy exchange.

Another man I slept with, someone who didn't have his life together at all but, again, who was magical in bed, brought me bad luck. I'd cut him off and then want to have sex with him again and, like clockwork, my flow would go awry. Weird, bad things would start happening in my life. This is how powerful energy exchange is with sex. You begin to carry their personality, thoughts, feeling, aura...all of it. So, ask yourself, "Does this person have a frequency that is healthy and positive?" If not, let that penis stroll on by. Monitor your sex life and keep shitty people out of your bed and your body. You can thank me later because this little nugget of information will change your life permanently. I also love condoms for this reason. They block some of that energy and keep you protected in ways that extend well beyond STDs.

While we're on the subject of sex, let's talk about when it's okay to sleep with someone so that you don't ruin your chances of having a relationship. I know that you're dying to know. Little lady, stop right there. Have I taught you nothing? This doesn't exist. Why? Because, again, I repeat and probably will again, rules in dating and relationships don't exist.

I've had long-term relationships with no less than three men I had sex with on the first night I met them. We totally fell in love. I'm not saying that always happens and I'm also not encouraging you to jump into bed with someone you don't know because of all the reasons I just stated. What I *am* saying is that sometimes sex really is an expression of an intense connection that exists for two people, one that is real and undeniable. I think it's more about how you handle the situation after you slept with the person right away. Are you brave enough to roll with it or are you going to call him immediately because you don't trust that he's really that into you? Or worse, are you going to play coy and wait for him to call so that you seem like the submissive, sweet girl? If YOU don't feel like talking, then don't. But if you think that sex was epic and you want more of him, kindly request that he get his ass over to your place because you are currently obsessed. And what happens if he doesn't respond or reciprocate? Who cares? You were you. If he wants to miss out on another episode of amazing connectedness and fun, then who is the one with the problem here? I don't think I need to tell you that it's him and not you. Next awesome guy, please.

We're Cyclical

I want to be clear so that some of you don't get lost—because I know how much you like to have a playbook, even though there isn't one. Everything I'm saying is to go after the guy you want, right? Be aggressive. Speak up. You are in charge. Wrong, that's not what I'm saying at all. I'm saying: Listen to your feelings. Sometimes it feels exactly right to express to the guy who just blew your mind that he blew your mind. Your body and mind will go, "Fuck! That was awesome. I need to see him again—now." And then, guess what? Maybe two days later you need space. You feel the need to focus on your work, write, draw, or paint, because all that sex has left you wanting something else. You're done blowing his head up. Suddenly your communication with him seems excessive and one-sided and you'd prefer he contact you. Or maybe you are itching to see that male friend of yours whom you don't want to sleep with at all.

Sound confusing? It is. And why does this happen? Because women are cyclical. Dear, life is cyclical. It's never always sunny. Sometimes it rains. Seasons exist. Men love to reference this behavior as games, or, worse, as women having some kind of personality disorder. "Oh shit," you say to yourself. "I can't be one of *those* women." Get over it. You're one of those women. You're one of those people. Funny, I never hear women say men are bi-polar when they feel the need to fuck outside their marriages or desire multiple sex partners. They just have stronger sexual appetites, right? Give me a break. I don't think I have to tell you that women can be sneaky as fuck and love having male attention and a variety of sex partners just as much as their male counterparts do. Let's all take a moment to congratulate the powers that be for justifying men being cyclical while shaming the fuck out of women. Good job guys, we fell for it and acted accordingly while you had all the fun.

Believe me, men are cyclical too, just not as cyclical, or as sensitive, as we are. (*In case you aren't clear about the definition of "sensitive", here it is: quick to detect or respond to slight changes, signals, or influences.)* Men have a tendency to operate linearly. They need things to be consistent, controlled, and safe. When women don't do the same, men are totally confused. Newsflash: guys, we don't have penises. We don't have as much testosterone. We aren't you. And many of you men who have a higher level of feminine energy understand what I'm talking about.

Uni-directional living is driven by masculinity and, because our society has been mostly determined by men, women—and men— have been forced to adapt to uni-directional living. I used to go around searching for the perfect place to live, the perfect job, etc. until I finally got smart and accepted that this kind of living didn't work for me at all, and it probably doesn't work for you either.

There was no one way for me. I'm bigger than that. I'm cyclical and expansive. I'm curious. I need it all. I need hot and cold, dark and light, north and south. Now, I'm not suggesting that you're as much of a gypsy-energy shifter as me, but I have a sneaking suspicion that most women are. The problem is that they've become convinced that it's wrong not to choose a direction or interest and stick with it until the end of time. I'm sure the psychology community has a field day with this. Better get into therapy because you can't choose or commit. There's something wrong with you.

For me, this thinking, and the freedom to choose, creates *balance*. I like having a job I can depend on, but I cannot be all work and no play. As I've already shared, I depend on artistic endeavors to balance the energy that goes into my job. I don't know how people can live static lives. I admire people who do, but I just feel there is so much out there to discover, especially now, so why in the world would someone want a redundant, mundane life? I'm not suggesting that having one partner is mundane. Having a romantic relationship can be a never-ending source of challenge, growth, and knowledge and also provide a range of about a zillion different emotions; however, maintaining balance in your relationship requires that you have interests outside of that relationship, independently. Let's hope he does also.

The spiritual community recognizes the five elements and the importance of building them into one's life to feel whole. They are fire, water, earth, air, and the ethereal. That's five pieces of your pie. That's a lot of slices, and each of those parts is complex and takes your energy, effort, and attention to engage with and incorporate into your life. Get to work on your pie so that you don't have to only look to a man to feel complete. He is (or they are) part of your dessert. Do you want to have a slice or the whole thing? And just imagine how expansive your life can be with a man who has his entire pie together and in balance. *Chills.*

Stop Talking

I forget where I saw it but in some weird spell book I owned and probably don't have anymore, I once read how important it is that, when casting a spell, to shut your damn mouth and not talk about it. And, truly, everything you are doing is spell casting. Just like sex needs awareness, so do the words you choose and who they are being spoken to.

Have you ever noticed that you have this one friend who, when you tell her about some exciting thing you have going on or some fabulous guy you just met that, shortly after, it all turns to shit? I have one particular friend who I sincerely watch what I say to, and it's mostly because she's much more grounded than me but has crazy witch powers; so, if she thinks what I'm saying is ridiculous, it gets in the way of my manifesting. It's not because she doesn't love me or is a bad friend, we just don't see life or men in the same way. Now, on the other hand, I have this friend I nick-named Glenda, an alien rockstar from another mother who I can't believe I met in this lifetime. If I tell her something I want, *poof*, it appears. Basically, if I share something with her, because she's on my vibe and wants nothing but top-level living for me, the energy behind that desire gets sent out exponentially.

For some reason, when I speak openly or in an excited manner about a guy I'm into, it blows up in my face. I think, for me, speaking about someone too early puts way too much expectation on the connection and my brain goes haywire. I've actually gotten really superstitious about all of this. My friends get a bit annoyed with me because I'll be dating someone for months and they will know nothing about it. Too bad. I don't want their opinions or their thought-based energy floating around in the air blocking mine. But I will definitely call in Glenda when I need some extra magic. Know your audience, or even better, shut the fuck up. How in the world does your girlfriend understand what's happening with your guy if you don't? Sit with your anxiety. Your anxiety about a situation is there to give you information. Fine, if you have to, call up someone you totally trust to send you good stuff and who will help you to get to the bottom of how you are feeling, but know that eventually you will figure it out and do exactly what's right for you. Some of the best advice I've ever gotten from a coach is this: *Unless it feels right, don't act.* Word.

Get an Advisor:
healer / coach / therapist / psychologist

The value of an advisor cannot, I repeat, cannot be overstated. Advisors come in many forms: healers, coaches, therapists, psychologists, and energy workers just to name a few. I have about three people on my speed dial whom I reach for to help me get to the bottom of my own truth. Note that I did not say advice. I don't need their fucking advice. But I *do* need them to tell me everything they objectively observe about what I'm sharing so that I can understand why I'm doing what I'm doing and to also assist me in breaking down patterns that no longer serve me. I need to understand why I'm feeling things. I don't know if you are the same, but I'm constantly examining myself and looking for a way to peel my own onion. Why do I do this?

Because I know that the more awareness and understanding I have about myself, the less I am driven by my own unconscious, self-sabotaging bullshit.

For instance, for a while, I could not shake an ex-boyfriend of mine. I couldn't figure out why I just couldn't keep myself from engaging with him, because I genuinely did not want to date or see him anymore. He's tough, pushy, and unreliable BUT also super playful via text and will entertain a woman because: A. He's financially supported by his family, so he works out a lot more than he works, giving him all the time in the world to fiddle on his phone; and B. He's narcissistic and loves female attention. He's also challenging and witty. So, I spent a good few months of my life trying to figure out why I couldn't stop engaging with him. I *needed* to understand why I was doing this. And, in the process, I couldn't stop beating myself up for not cutting him off. So, guess what? Months later, when I was on the phone with one of my goddess coaches, she helped me to realize that, when my ex was in my life, I was more creative. Like, crazy creative. I felt alive.

Shortly after, I met other more artsy men and stopped engaging with him, but another key to me releasing the connection was that I had made peace with what I was doing. I stopped judging myself and resisting my choice, so he floated away because I let him. In that session, after more than forty years of my life, I finally realized that having connections with men makes me feel inspired. They are my muses. A lack of male energy makes me feel dead. I don't write. I don't draw. I watch television until my eyes cross. It basically sucks. Just like Picasso needed women around to paint, men inspire me and help me to draw on the sacral energy from which creative energy is born. I recognize the importance of engaging with them for creativity. *A major driving force in my creative life is male energy,* and this light bulb went off for me all because I was humble enough to work with another gifted human being.

Working with an advisor can be tricky. Incompetent people and frauds practice in the healing arts just like they do in every industry. Actually, studies show that many therapists choose their professions because they are, in fact, co-dependents themselves. For every advisor who has changed my life and provided me with heightened awareness, healing, and priceless bits of wisdom, I've found at least three others who I wished I hadn't worked with. For example, I once had a therapist tell me that I collect men. Is that judgmental and shaming or what? This particular therapist had helped me with some childhood wounding and work issues, but she also encouraged me to stay in a borderline abusive relationship because she had me convinced the red flags I was seeing were deep-seated issues I needed to deal with. In this case, they weren't. Another had me so fearful of a man I was dating that I left the country for a week. Essentially, despite their good intentions, these two therapists left me feeling disempowered. The first one I mentioned sincerely made me feel badly about myself. She even attempted to text me after I ended our sessions, which is highly inappropriate and could have resulted in her losing her license.

After working with a ton of coaches and spiritual healers, what I have learned is that it is vitally important that you do not give your power away to these people. Yes, they are educated in their field—sometimes—but they are human. It is virtually impossible to advise others without allowing one's own personal experiences to inform sessions meant to uncover another's truth. Your truth is different from mine. A good advisor will allow you to guide the sessions and invite you to think and process on your own. They will *not* attempt to disempower you so that you become dependent on them. They also shouldn't attach to you or make you feel badly about moving on. As you grow and evolve you will likely discover that advisors who once felt great to work with no longer feel like a good fit. This is your life. You have the right to fuck it up and you are also the person responsible for you. Also, please remember that as humans we have the habit of embellishing our personal stories. While working with advisors, do your best to share your experiences honestly so that those who are truly talented at healing can help you to be magnificent, healthy, and wise.

In case you aren't a person who has sought assistance in managing your life outside of the realm of therapists and psychologists, let me introduce you to some of my healing posse. I think sharing specifics about who I have most recently worked with, none of whom are therapists and psychologists, might allow some of you to have a better idea about the kinds of magic and knowledge healers and coaches are capable of providing. Let me also add that *all* of these people work by phone or virtually, so your location has nothing to do with finding a suitable advisor.

Example one: my law of attraction coach/ wizard. Let's call him The Wizard for fun because, after I started working with him as a law of attraction coach, he started dabbling in wizardry in much the same way Harry Potter does and, let me add, he was fucking phenomenal at it.

I call The Wizard when I see my external reality repeating itself or find myself trapped in a loop. Ladies, most of the time I can shift almost anything but, if I can't, and I know something is off with me, this is the dude I look to. He has also given me some metaphysical tools to add to my bag of tricks because, coincidentally (or not, because I don't believe in coincidence in the least), I started reading about the metaphysical world and studying magic after meeting him but before he had incorporated those same modalities into his work. The Wizard strengthened my practice.

Example two: my life coach. I fucking hate the whole concept of a "life coach" and I also hate the phrase "life coach" but, honestly, that's what she is. Look, after working with this woman for a few years now I still haven't figured out how she helps me to shift my life; she just does. She has a talent for getting me to the essence of who I am and what it is that I want. She hones in on authenticity. She's gifted at pinpointing and putting into words how I'm feeling when I'm out of sorts and encourages me to capitalize on my true nature, but, more importantly, to absolutely love that nature, even if it's at odds with the mainstream. I want you to think about the kind of love and goodness that has to exist inside of another person to help someone in that way. Not *once*, in more than two years, have I caught her judging me or projecting. She's a clean soul and clean souls are fucking rare. Call someone like her into your life if you haven't already because, take it from me, you need a person like this on your side.

Example three: my spiritual mother. I want to tell you that you will find someone like my spiritual mother but, honestly, I think this person is so unusually gifted in what she does that I can't imagine two of her being in the world. She and I are approaching two decades of working together. In short, meeting her changed my life. She put me on the spiritual path I live on today. My spiritual mother channels, sees angels, and is a reiki master. I don't live near her anymore but I used to receive reiki with her at least once a month. Now, I call her when I want a little information from the unseen or when I'm having an issue reading another person's soul. She taught me how to access my own spiritual gifts, like clairvoyance and clairaudience, ones I knew I had but had been blocking because of the way I was raised. I can read energy. I can read people. I can hear messages other people can't. I know some of you think I sound a bit crazy sharing this but, darling, believe it. Those who know me also know that what I just shared with you isn't bullshit. It's also another reason Katie wanted me to write this book for you.

I want to pause and warn you a bit about those who work with the unseen. Ladies, anyone can study anything but some individuals are just natural healers. Energy work, tarot reading, and channeling are serious stuff. To give you an example, after this woman would channel for me or perform reiki, I would get the chills, almost like I had the flu, within a half-hour of leaving her. The high I had from my sessions would last almost a week. She would create massive shifts for me when I needed them, almost instantaneously. Can you imagine if you worked with someone with this kind of power who didn't have good intentions? Be especially discerning of those who work with the esoteric.

Advisors are invaluable but please always remember that you don't need fixed. My love, you are perfect in every way. Others are meant to help us grow. They aren't meant to turn us into cookie-cutter, sheep followers. Keep your essence no matter who you work with or know. Everyone you meet—including soulmates and the loves of your life—comes in to enhance what you already have…and to heal what needs healing.

The Goddess Myth

Be careful when you first begin dating a man because, for the most part, in the beginning, men are enamored, which is not to be confused for love. Sure, these romantic feelings seem completely real for them, but what they don't know is they are setting you up for failure because most men subscribe to the goddess myth. Now ladies, don't go getting mad at men. They can't help that, initially, they see you as superhuman and flawless.

So, what is the goddess myth? The goddess myth is based around the premise that he's decided you are *perfect* and that your dark side doesn't possibly exist, even though it exists for everyone. He believes you are different. He's met the one woman in the world who isn't going to give him a hard time, is easy-going, gorgeous, and totally together.

Huh? *Of fucking course* you are going to be giving him a hard time! You're a woman.

We scream and yell. We become enraged over dirty dishes while holding our families together when our guy loses his job or, worse, ends up in jail or another woman's bed; except, we cried and screamed the MOST over the dishes. We make no sense and will continue to make no sense until the end of time, but many men still want to believe in the illusion of the perfect female, because somewhere along the way they got confused—too many Tarzan and Star Wars movies, maybe. Or, possibly, because their mamas looked at them with adoration after their sweet munchkins lit the couch on fire or pulled down their pants and took a piss in the corner. They just stared up at their mothers in awe. Her love was unconditional. Well, you're not his mama, and the bathroom is for pissing.

We're not about blaming other women for our dating problems, right? No way. Real goddesses don't blame others, including men, for the obstacles they encounter. Instead, they find solutions.

The secret to working around the goddess myth is to be authentic and to refuse to perpetuate a myth that has been repressing women, especially inside of their relationships, since the beginning of time. I know, I know, I keep telling you to just BE YOURSELF, and then, just maybe, you try to convince yourself that I'm crazy and unaware of things women are "supposed" to do to get a man.

We're far enough along now that I hope you're in a headspace to know that you don't need bait to attract a man...THE man. I also hope that you're catching on to the basic concept of becoming the you that is closest to your true essence, and the importance of showing your true colors to the world, so that you'll attract men and, well, people of all kinds who belong in your life. We want all those douchebags you wish you had never met to just float away and to stop coming your way. I want you to become the real you so that they *never* want you and are repelled by you.

You are not a myth, but a goddess? You bet. Goddesses have rough edges, flaws, and sweetness. They are also *magnetic*

Be Magnetic

I have a couple of girlfriends whom I love dearly, but when I watch them interact with men I want to turn into a murderous bitch. I want to slap them in the face or stab them right in the eye and say: "Beautiful girl!! Can you just PLEASE stop reaching, needing, and generally throwing yourself at any man with a pulse?" The reason their behavior bothers me so much is because I see them as having the possibility of being irresistible to the opposite sex. The problem is...they don't see it in themselves.

Desperation is not a good look; it's also not who you are. Flirting and dating require practice and are an art. Those who are the most gifted at the art of attraction understand that *magnetism* is their secret weapon. They also know that men are VERY perceptive and able to tell the difference between interest and neediness. Men can easily spot a woman who is whole versus another who is incomplete. Incomplete women push because they don't believe a man will come to them, in the same way a baby runs to candy. Incomplete women dominate conversations instead of talking and listening. Magnetic women are not in a conversation to *get* anything. They have what they need. A magnetic woman converses with a man while being mindful of whether or not he's worthy of *her* and *her time*. She might also just be there to have fun and entertain herself. She's in the moment. She knows that when she enters the room, she is beautiful. She doesn't need anyone to tell her so.

Women can be unconscious of their need for attention and validation, and I would be a hypocrite if I didn't admit that, in the past, I have been one of those women and, occasionally, still can be because I'm human. But needing to be externally validated is dangerous and that's mostly because, as I've already stated, if you need something outside of yourself to feel good, then you're basically fucked. Let me expand on this...

When you develop a dependence on a man to see, choose, validate, or notice you then you also give him the power to shake or shatter you if he leaves. This also means that you are one step short of being an addict. The requirement of a man's attention turns us into women we are not and forces us to compromise when it isn't good for us. This kind of behavior also drains us of our vital energy; we become less of who we were designed to be because, if someone has the ability to take away the blanket you think you need to feel whole, then you are going to do all kinds of things that are beneath you to keep from losing it. To have love and to experience a healthy relationship means that you love that person, and yourself, whether they stay or go. That's the difference between true love as opposed to dependency. That's also the difference between having self-respect versus having none.

I think most of us desire companionship, but for most people, this is based on an external need that has yet to be met or identified by the internal self. Why do you need to be desired and validated by a man to know you are attractive? Better get to the bottom of that. Why do you need to be fucked to know you are fuckable? Same thing. The pressure that has been put upon women by society to be married and have children to be seen as worthy is immense. Despite most marriages not working at all, many women still believe that their lives just can't be complete if they don't have a husband or children. If you feel that way, spend some time with your married friends. They are the best people to dispel this principle for you. Some of them dream of a time when they could be single, selfish, and free again. But the best reason to spend time with your married friends and those who are in long-term relationships is to keep you connected to the reality of being in their situation. They are going to keep you grounded in the truth about relationships and marriage: that they can be *tough* and take *work*.

I sincerely love the romantic notion of being married, but if you are driven to obtain a husband, ask yourself why. Is it to feel "normal" and prove to everyone that someone loves you enough to marry you? Fear of abandonment can also be a catalyst for choosing to marry rather than simply valuing a relationship. No matter your feelings about marriage and relationships, fall in love with your own life so that someone can complement it; a husband isn't a substitute for inner work.

Send yourself flowers, baby goddess. Take yourself to the movies. Buy a great vibrator. Give yourself everything within your power that you *think* you need from a man so that it's one less need you have, providing you with the ability to appreciate the human sitting opposite you for nothing more than their amazing company and being generally fucking awesome. Oh, and while you're at it, get a great J-O-B. You want a man so that you can be taken care of financially? No one ever gained inner strength by depending on a man for money. I'm not saying you need to run out and go to medical school. And I'm also not saying that you need to make more money than your guy. But if you can't stand on your own two feet financially if you had to, then you are essentially placing yourself in a position of powerlessness. And, if you are reading this book, I'm assuming you're looking for a partner and not a pimp. Harsh? Yes, and stated harshly to make sure you *stay woke.*

If you know, to your very core, that you are amazing and worthy of love, then you just are...period. And, voila, you become magnetic to the opposite sex. Correction. You become magnetic to practically everyone and love of all kinds finds you. And, not to brag, but I *promise* you this is why men approach me all the time. I'm magnetic and I know it. I don't go looking for a man. I don't try to get their attention. If they need me to do this then, as far as I'm concerned, they aren't for me. They are for some other woman they find magnetic...or maybe they just don't like blondes.

Keep Your Shit Tight

It's time for another terrifying dating tale, and this one, luckily, is not about me. And do you know why it isn't about me? It's because I keep my shit tight. There is ONE, count 'em ONE, man on the planet who has a picture of me in lingerie. It was taken in my twenties and it's a Polaroid and probably in the trash or some secret safety deposit box that I assume he visits once a quarter because he's married now. And, quite frankly, if it got out, I'd probably be over the moon because I can't imagine that photo doing anything but raising my rep given how hot I was in my late twenties. But, even then, I wasn't dumb enough to take nudes and give them to men.

Calm down! I'm not a prude. I'm not above sending sexy photos to a man, but here's the question I always ask myself before I do: "Would it bother me if this got out and the world saw it?" So, as long as I look amazing and nothing super-personal is shown, then, yeah, every now and then I'll throw my man a bone. Notice I wrote "my man" and not some guy I'm trying to seduce by objectifying myself so that he will take an interest in me.

Unfortunately, you younger cookies and even some of you older ones not only trust others to protect your privacy, because you've forgotten that love is transient and that your dream guy can turn into your most-hated enemy in a flash, but you also don't send photos or videos *mindfully*.

While we're on this subject can you please just take those photos of you with your BFF holding your beer bong offline? Yes, every savvy business owner is searching the internet before we interview you for a job, and the moment we see pictures like the one I just referenced or low-class statements on social media, we throw your resume in the trash. We want intelligent women who also look like they are together enough to be associated with the companies we worked our asses off to create, but I digress…

The story I'm about to tell you is about a woman who once worked for me and whom I love to pieces. In this case, her romantic partner was female. However, I don't think anyone reading this would disagree that a man, or woman who wishes she had your man, is completely capable of ruining your psychological and emotional well-being, not to mention your reputation, by accessing your phone and/or social media.

This horrifying story began to unfold a few days after this couple's third, or fourth, or fifth, break-up. I can't remember the details. I received a DM from a person unknown to me warning me that I shouldn't be employing this girl. Really nasty stuff. A second message flies into the inbox of her other employer and there it went. Over the course of the next year and a half, her life periodically became a living hell. Her emails were hacked. Her photos were hacked. Her social media was hacked. And, to make matters worse, her next relationship ended with explicit photos and videos of her and her most recent partner being posted to social media *from their own accounts,* and without their consent, because neither of them could get into the accounts to shut them down. Friends and family watched in horror while these two women's most intimate moments together were plastered all over the internet for the world to see.

To date, this friend of mine and former employee has had her life terrorized at least three times in less than two years. If the person couldn't hack her, then they would find ways to contact her on a cell, or through whatever e-mail they could find, to tell her how awful she was and encourage her to end her life. Now, I don't care if you're a woman made of steel, you're going to get fucked in the head if that shit happens to you. And do you know what the police said after she had filed her SIXTH police report? Why aren't you off social media? Read that again. So, please, I beg of you, protect yourself. Think about what you are doing. Keep your shit tight so that you are in control of your image and life. Let's not allow the sociopaths of the world to fuck with us if we can help it.

Here are a few more tidbits to hammer my "...keep your shit tight..." mantra into your head...

Another friend of mine kept racy photos of her and her ex under her bed. Her live-in boyfriend found them and broke up with her. Once, while I was in Hawaii, a boyfriend of mine, who was supposed to be feeding my dog and not snooping, managed to find my personal journal in my pillowcase and read it cover to cover. He didn't enjoy the parts about me fantasizing about screwing my workout partner and he especially didn't find the detailed account of what a shit I thought he was particularly amusing, even though the latter was written while we were on a break—I think. Lock up your photos and diaries and password protect anything you want kept private.

As women, we often feel like we need to share the truth and nothing but the truth to have integrity. I beg to differ. Not everyone deserves to know the truth about our lives; sometimes our privacy and safety has to take precedence over honesty. No one, unless you want them to, should know what goes on in your bedroom with the local drug dealer who has the emotional intelligence the size of a pea and a cock that resembles Mt. Everest. Also, if you can help it, try to never put things in writing you wouldn't want others to see.

You'll thank me later. After all, if you don't, it's your word against his and, *actually, since you asked, I've never even seen that guy's dick, but thanks for stopping by.* Small town girls, I know protecting your privacy is more of a challenge, but you've got this! You can always move or get some strange while on vacation if you need it. You don't owe it to the world to explain your every move. Strangers and acquaintances haven't earned the right to have access to your intimate life. Knowing you is a privilege and your boundaries are put in place for a reason.

Grey Sucks

I don't know about you, but I hate grey. Don't get me wrong, I'm a big fan of grey being in my wardrobe where it rightfully belongs; however, when it comes to my relationships and even my business, grey makes me climb the walls. For me, grey is this in-between-no-mans-land I enter when someone around me is hiding something or when I don't know which road to take. When grey comes rolling into my brain like a cloud, I begin to lose my patience and my mind. This seemingly unassuming, insignificant shade triggers me and my brain starts whispering, *"Bitch, time to get more information."* And, I can promise you, one way or another, I'm going to get it.

Let me tell you how, I believe, weak and insecure people feel about grey. THEY. LOVE. IT. They will sit in this non-confrontational, neutral hue forever because it means they don't have to get real and can avoid being responsible until the end of time, or they are scared shitless of being open and honest because being direct means facing you and/or themselves. Grey also allows wimps to never make a choice. There's nothing to lose, or gain, for that matter, in grey.

I get it. Grey is comfy and black or white is scary. But how many times have you felt relieved after you got the real story, even if it was bad? Why? Because you could make a choice based on reality and get on with your life, that's why. Shady people—those who gravitate to grey—are skilled at keeping others' worlds dull and murky. *Ick*. Are you feeling me with why I think grey is shitty? Just don't be pissed at me when you get the truth. I love truth. Truth is where I like to curl up and live.

I feel, to prove my point, we need an example here...

While still in my twenties, I was madly in love with a man for a solid two years. He was irritatingly smoldering...smart...hot...*ugh*. He and I were completely obsessed with one another. And I think most sane people would agree that, when you don't want to leave the other person's side for even a second and just the sight of their arm makes you want to take your clothes off and forget about the rest of the world, then, well, there's about to be trouble. He and I would hole up in his place for weekends at a time. We'd pass out, make love, repeat. Basic necessities became secondary to us fucking. We'd take bathroom breaks and snack on cereal in bed between orgasms until finally, wow, it's 10 p.m., maybe we should shower and go have a meal. I think I've made my point here. Um, we were sexual.

Unfortunately, when we met, he was involved with someone else. His girlfriend lived in another country, so, clearly, I wasn't too concerned at the time, but shortly after we started seeing each other, he broke up with her anyway per my insistence. *Great.* Except, after about a year into our "committed" relationship, I became tortured. We were completely volatile…breaking up every other week then fucking and making up. And always, in the back of mind, he was cheating. All kinds of things happened to make me believe this that I'm not going to get into here, but what bothered me the most about our scenario was the following: I was living in grey. I didn't know what the fuck was happening until one day I saw a phone number, while I was secretly going through his phone, that I didn't recognize. The other girlfriend and I had about an hour-long phone call realizing he was playing us both.

He had even gone so far as to get a different cell phone (a matching pair, so that they looked identical) for each of us to call. After the conversation with the other woman, I never spoke to that piece of shit again because, well, I'm not insane, but mostly because I had finally gotten out of grey, knew what was going on, and, even though I was broken-hearted, had the information I needed to move on.

In addition to seeing why grey is a color to avoid, via my cautionary tale, I think we can also agree that karma exists. I got mine, but I also learned a valuable lesson in love, one I have never forgotten, about staying out of grey. I was also forced to learn the hard way to never ignore my intuition. The moment you start investigating or going through your man's garbage (Yes, I did that too.) just know that you're doing it for a reason. So, whenever you can, stay out of grey. Life is a lot better when you're surrounded by those who live their lives in color.

Action is Everything

Can we believe how easy it has become for men to drain our energy and capture our attention? If we could go back in time wouldn't we have VERY strong conversations with the masterminds who invented texting? Or, maybe we would find a way to lock up Mark Zuckerberg before he turned eighteen. We'd put him on a deserted island with armed guards (women, of course) allowing him basic food and water, with no access to the internet, while coming up with a very different idea on how to change the world as we know it. This way we could guarantee that Facebook, the literal devil that started the evolution of social media, would never have been birthed. We might also have suggested to Steve Jobs that there be some kind of restriction put on texting that forces a man to call occasionally. Fine, I know these brilliant men had every intention of uniting us globally and are MENSA-level smart, but their inventions have impacted the dating world in a negative way and have also forced us into masturbation sessions that might qualify us as sex addicts.

I'm here to tell you that, unfortunately, dating was *A LOT* better before texting and social media came along. If a man wanted to get to know you, go up your skirt, or down your pants, then he had to make plans. Essentially, if a guy wanted to get the girl, or even a blow job, he had to take ACTION. He also couldn't sit on his lazy ass going through his phone texting five different women, "You up?" or "Wanna come over?" to see who would bite.

Does the change in the dating landscape, like the use of cell phones, social media of all kinds, and "Goodness, what the fuck will they come up with next?" alter the way you handle yourself with men. NO. NO. And, in case you missed the latter, NO! Your standards are your standards...doesn't matter if we all move to the moon and send messages from the antennas on our heads.

Men have a pretty hard time selling me their lazy, weird, sexting behavior because I've seen the other side. Statements I've heard from these guys include, but are not limited to, the following: "You're too difficult...You're cold...You play games." I run hot and cold with these men because I respond to action and behavior I prefer and ignore shit I want no part of. Does that make me difficult? Probably. Why do I stand my ground and keep it moving when they don't take action? Because I've experienced what men are capable of doing when they want you. Once you've visited "the kingdom of men who take action", you're not settling for anything less.

I know it's probably difficult to believe men can take action, especially if you're in your twenties and haven't seen the proof, but don't think that just because you're dealing with younger men you're unable to be escorted by them to said kingdom. My ex-husband was a man of action before he was old enough to legally drink, so, no, your guy doesn't have the excuse of lack of experience, finances, or general ignorance. If he's over thirty and not taking action and you insist on keeping him around DESPITE HIM OBVIOUSLY SHOWING YOU THAT HE CAN'T TAKE ACTION RIGHT FROM THE BEGINNING by getting you to pop over to his house or work to "hang out" or even by manipulating you into making him bi-weekly dinners (you "nice" girl), then just hand him the remote because that scene from the couch is the one you'll be witnessing...forever. While you're making most of the money, cooking, doing the dishes, and raising the kids, he'll still be wondering why you're nagging at him to do so much as drive the newborn to daycare. Why? Why not?! You showed him you were fine with him not taking action from the start. *Them's the rules, kid.*

Talk is cheap. People interested in real connection show up and follow through. True relationships, and friendships, are born out of effort. If you see that a man isn't meeting you at least half-way, keeps you on the hook with his sweet texts or words while doing nothing more, or convinces you to take all the action and risk for the two of you to be together, then get out. He's never changing. He might even mean well and wish he could do more, but if he can't, then he just can't. These kinds of men have left me feeling irritated, vexed, and generally murderous more than any other guys on the planet. I *WISH* I could get back the days, and even months, wasted on them so that I could have done other really important things...like floss, deep condition my hair, or visually digest more trashy magazines.

I'm not suggesting you sit back and say nothing while he texts. Men have fragile egos and fear of rejection is very real for them. Find ways to tell the man you're interested in that you want to talk or see each other, then let him figure out the rest. If he can't, then he's not the guy for you.

The Villains

I don't want to upset you, but I have something VERY important to tell you: *fucked-up people exist*. I know, I can't believe it either. The worst part is that many of them have a penis.

I want you to date the good guys. I want them to be passionate about their lives, soulful, kind, and fearless, so I'm going to take the liberty—because I care about you so very much—to warn you about a very specific type of man. Without further ado, allow me to introduce...the personality-disordered male. OMFG, the horror.

Actually, while I was writing this, another fifty, nearly human men just crossed over, so I'd better hop to it. Right this very moment—somewhere in the world—a narcissist is sitting at a coffee shop eyeing a girl who just rolled up in her own Range Rover. He's already dreaming of moving into the mansion she built—with her own blood, sweat, and tears—while he searches: "ways to access a woman's bank account without her noticing". Elsewhere, a man is leaning over a bar, looking deep into the sparkling eyes of a woman whose only familiarity with *Borderline* is Madonna. "Can you imagine how beautiful your skin would look next to mine?" rolls off of his tongue. Oh yes, that last line once went straight from a man's mouth directly to my ears; I fell for it, and him, because I didn't have a woman warning me about the obvious red flags that accompany unhealthy men. Lucky for you, I'm here now.

The narcissist and the borderline don't want me to tell you their secrets but I'm going to anyway because, well, you already know whose side I'm on. They are people who, until they have found ways to break their patterns and overcome their lack of vulnerability, use others as objects in an effort to feel whole. Both of these men have emotional voids and unstable personalities that can only be healed with therapy and inner work, but, until they wake up—which is sometimes never— they will be reaching for women like you and wreaking havoc on your life as a consequence. Sound scary? Yes.

These men have two VERY distinct characteristics. The first is that they will come at you as feverishly as a blood-thirsty vampire. Why? Because they are on the look-out for immediate gratification and, also, because they are hoping you won't have time to use that big brain of yours. If you did, then you'd figure out: 1. He is not who he says he is; and 2. He doesn't give an actual shit about you. I know you're fabulous but if someone is calling or texting you ten times a day in the first week or sending you nude photos before learning your last name, then pay attention because, chances are, you're dealing with a personality-disordered male.

Here's the second major red flag: mirroring. He'll immediately drop words like "twin". He's just like you, right? You've found your soulmate. *Wrong*. He is the ultimate chameleon. If you tell him you love clowns, suddenly he was in the circus or plans to be in one. *Where the fuck did that come from?* He's about to have his big break and he's got the contract to prove it. *Wrong again, dear. He's homeless, which is why he's trying to stay over every night.* Is that last bit an excerpt from a bad movie? Nope. It happened to one of my closest friends. After she found out his real story, he trashed her apartment and smashed her television. Really? The TV?!! I don't know about you, but I can't live without well-crafted media streaming through my television for more than half a day…and that's only if there's an abundance of wine in the house.

So, what should you do when you meet these men? Call them out? Try to change them? Please don't. Send them love (telepathically) and move along. You don't need to try to rescue or save anyone. You also don't need to put yourself at risk by making a point. We are all responsible for our own healing. You've got your hands full managing your own gigantic, magical life, so save *yourself*. Yes, I understand that disordered men are people too but, my dear, let's not waste your compassion on those who currently have none. A man who has no idea who he is or what he stands for needs to be let go because, at minimum, we want people in our lives who are taking their meds when indicated.

The Married Man

Please don't judge me, but I've been taken in by a married man a few times; however, I'm really happy I did the research for you and excited to report that almost all of these guys use the same ammo, allowing you to avoid them like the fucking plague, which is what you should do, *no exceptions*.

I realize that some women stick it out and diminish themselves for the hope of a relationship by waiting around for these dickheads, but don't do it. One of my best friends managed to land herself a married man in her early twenties. Their wedding was even more glorious than his first. And guess what? I'm sure you're shocked to learn that the love of my friend's life cheated on her a few years into their marriage. Lesson learned. And let's not even get into how disrespectful you are being to the other woman. It took me some growing up to realize that, yes, just because I didn't start the relationship (all of the married men I dated pursued me and lied to me about being married in the beginning) and I wasn't the married one, I still owed it to other women to be respectful.

The worst thing about meeting a married man is how devastatingly attractive they are because they carry a grown-up, responsible vibe that many single guys just don't have because they are still acting like children. We meet them, and we tell ourselves it's okay. They remind us of our daddies.

Married men can be slick if you aren't careful because they are smart enough to hook you first, get you to fall in love, and then confess. They know that once they start sleeping with you and have your heart on a stick, it's going to be a trillion times more difficult for you to leave. Please, for your sake, cut it off the moment you know. The only person benefitting by you staying is him. If someone is lying to their partner, are they really a good person? Obviously not. Your fabulousness didn't make him do it. His inability to man-up and deal with the issues in his marriage and take responsibility for himself did. You aren't the first person he's cheated with and you won't be the last. He feels justified because his wife is at home holding him accountable and they have turned into friends more than lovers. She stopped feeding his ego a long time ago. *That's marriage, duh.*

As I stated, almost all married men have the same story. You'd think there would be some variation but there rarely is. Every one of them I've ever met, whether I've gotten involved with them or not, says the same thing once I find out: "We're just in it for the kids. We stopped sleeping together a long time ago and it's complicated." Well, he might be complicated, but she probably isn't and is at home thinking her marriage is just fucking fine. Why do single women go along with this? Because we have been brainwashed into thinking we should be nurturing and understanding. "Oh, those poor babies and poor him. He needs us. She sounds terrible." *Stop.*

Not long ago I met a guy on a flight to New York who had all the promise of my dream guy. No wedding ring and shows me pictures of his kids with no images of a woman. We exchange numbers in first class and then he starts mad texting me for an entire week. Once Saturday rolls around, he disappears. Ladies, if a man goes as quiet as a mouse in the evenings and on weekends, or shifts his texting patterns during these hours, then your radar needs to go off. It took about five minutes for a friend of mine and me to find some evidence of his marriage online. When I asked him if he was married and notified him that I didn't feel comfortable texting a married man, even if it was just for some friendly banter, here's what he said: "Haha, friendly banter. I like your wit. Long story." *Wow, motherfucker, I didn't see what was funny or witty about that question.* And I guess I also didn't get the memo about the *"Are you married?"* question being a long story. It's one word: yes or no. Simple and easy, but these tricky dicks would love for you to think otherwise. I never responded. A few days later he texted me again wanting to know if he had said something inappropriate. *No, you're inappropriate,* not to mention shady as fuck. The end. He's lucky I didn't send the entire thread to his wife.

Am I sounding a little hypocritical here because I did cheat on my husband? Yes, and what a child I was for exhibiting such ridiculous behavior. Good thing for me I started dealing with my own issues instead of continuing to subject an innocent person to my own garbage. Every person you know deserves better, especially you.

Don't date a married man. He's not leaving his wife. He can tell you he loves you all day, but he doesn't. If he did, then he wouldn't subject you to such degrading behavior in the first place. And if his marriage ever does actually dissolve—probably because she got smarter—you're never going to trust him because you can't. We've got better things to suffer over than a dead-end and someone else's sloppy seconds.

The
Man-Child

Let me tell you something else I've realized from dating a lot of men. *ALERT. ALERT.* Politically incorrect statement ahead. Back away slowly from this book if biased statements offend, even if they are completely based on thirty years of research gathered through my personal dating experiences and are the actual fucking truth...most of the time.

A guy who grows up without a masculine role-model or influence often thinks he deserves to be treated like a king, rather than a partner, while in a relationship with a woman. He's also *highly likely* to take next to zero responsibility for the role he plays in creating conflict that may arise inside of that relationship. Essentially, he thinks this because he didn't witness true relationship dynamics (which he could have even seen while being raised by same-sex parents). Unless he was in the minority and was raised by a woman who had a highly evolved sense of self-respect, a powerful job, and extremely balanced masculine and feminine energy, he thinks that he is entitled to all of the perks of a woman without contributing shit. Oops. Did I just say that men who grow up in a single-parent household raised by a woman will VERY LIKELY want you to be their mother rather than take on the responsibility of being your partner? *Yes, I said it. And, guurrrrl, I'm gonna say it again.*

Obviously, no one should be so narrow-minded to take a group of people and assume that coming from the same set of circumstances makes them all the same, but when those circumstances shape and mold how one perceives relationships then, well, attention must be paid. So, enter with caution if your guy was abandoned by his father.

Look, I'm not talking about a man who, like many of the men in the world, grew up with divorced parents or with a stepfather who came along after biological daddy skipped out before anyone could ever remember his name. I'm talking about a man who spent the majority of his formative years without a man in the house, surrounded by his lovely mom and maybe even his grandmama. Lovely ladies, I'm really sorry if you're reading this right now and feel shamed by me for telling you that your son, *who you're raising all by your damn self because men can be shit and, yeah, I know you don't need a man to do it, damnit.*

But—the thing is—until recently, most women haven't been empowered enough by society to take on such a task and not feel guilty about it, so they attempted to give their sons the world to compensate for the absence of a father. These women didn't have the emotional support they needed and, more than often, also didn't have the financial support they needed, so little Billy got the bright idea that he was going to be the man of the house, even though he had no reason to be, without contributing to the finances or even volunteering to do the dishes.

In some cases, it gets worse, because occasionally these mothers treated their sons like husbands. So, there they were, trying to be kids, while mom's lack of support made these little boys feel as though they were overly responsible for mom's happiness. *Boom.* Enter the aversive, non-committal man who is scared shitless of losing himself in a relationship, has never learned to face conflict with a woman, and runs from one superficial romance to another. Essentially, this guy got exposed solely to feminine energy. He never learned or experienced the masculine within his household, which is a lot more likely for a kid growing up now, because, yeah, women are becoming more encouraged each and every day to be and do it all, allowing them— all by themselves—to raise tiny humans who grow up to be badass adults who can take on anything.

Why does the field of psychology have no problem saying that children who were abused are more likely to become abused by their partners, or, worse, have a higher chance of becoming abusers, but doesn't have the guts to point out the detriments of men who grow up without being exposed to masculine energy. I'm saying it. Take note. Put it in your psychology textbooks and, if you're a man reading this, get into therapy and figure your shit out. No woman wants to be your mama. She's not giving you unconditional love. That's what a parent does. Your girl comes with conditions and these conditions mean you're giving to the relationship, in one way or another, as much as she does.

Conversion of the Manfriend

Katie specifically requested I write this section, so I'm doing it with extreme trepidation because I'm mortified that she would ever give a shit about *trying* to get some guy who can't recognize her goddess position in life instead of trapping her in the friend zone, but I'm playing along here because I know there are more Katies out there. Plus, I do kind of owe her for convincing me that I needed to write this book. So, here we go...

How do you get your manfriend out of the friend zone and into dreamy boyfriend-land? Here's the long and short of it—*BITCH, YOU CAN'T.* Let it go. Oh sure, once you're over him and with Mr. Amazing he'll suddenly confess his undying love for you, but seriously? Are we looking for someone who needs another guy to give us attention before he can recognize the fabulousness we possess? I think not. And, just so you know, because some friend of yours is going to get sassy and say, "Don't listen to her!!! Honey, do you see this rock on my finger? That's exactly how I nabbed my husband," I'm going to expand on this. Oh yes, shitty friend, I accept your challenge.

This is exactly how I ended up with my perfect husband. Perfect in every way except for the fact that we never had sex, like ever. And why do I think this was? Because we were *friends*, like the best of friends, for almost a year before we were romantic. He never saw me as the sexy minx that I am. He never had to pursue me or date me UNTIL the man that I had been talking about incessantly for an entire summer, and who I was also crazy over, came to visit me. Suddenly, the man who barely paid me a compliment (and rarely paid me a compliment once I was his wife), was suddenly in love with me. So in love, according to him, that he gave me an ultimatum: be my girlfriend or we're no longer going to be friends.

To be clear, my ex-husband was the best in many aspects. I was with him almost every day when we were friends. Back then I couldn't have imagined my life without him, even though I was in love with someone else, a man I still recall as one of the sweetest most delicious boyfriends I've ever had. So, what did I do? I left the long-distance boyfriend whom I was going to marry, and the rest is history. I married my buddy a few years later and I was miserable. Why? Well, one of the many reasons was that he never saw me as his lover. I was a conquest. He was a big shot. He could have had almost any woman he wanted, but his best friend—me—wasn't giving him the time of day romantically. He chose me because I was someone to be conquered. Once that happened, I was just another addition to his many accomplishments.

I bitched and moaned the majority of our relationship. He never listened or gave a shit...until...I started sleeping with another man and left him three months later. Suddenly he cared again. Ladies, that's not love; that's ego. And even though I had a gorgeous ring, Mr. Perfect, and the big wedding of every girl's dream, that marriage was the loneliest time of my life. Don't get me wrong, having a friendship with your partner is an important aspect of a great relationship, but don't fall for the guy who only loves you after you belong to someone else. It's not real and never will be.

The Penis Problem

Let's get one thing straight. His penis problem is not yours. Well, you can make it your problem if you like, but I don't like to make it mine. I can't begin to tell you how many men I've met who do weird shit so that I won't know one of their dirty little secrets, which includes, but is not limited to: his tiny penis, his inability to perform, or the fact that he ejaculates once he's near a vagina. When I say I don't like to make it my problem, I don't mean that I don't date these guys. Honestly, I almost married a guy with a small penis because our sex became incredible and we worked around it. What I do mean is: Don't let a guy project his penis problems onto you, because, unfortunately, that's what many of them will do. He'll make every excuse in the book not to let you know about his malfunction until he's got you looking and feeling crazy because you've gotten too close to intimacy with him. Let me tell you a sad story…

I had a crush on an Adonis-like creature. I used to break out in hives when he jumped into the elevator of my building where he also lived. He looked like a young Jared Leto: about 6'2", drove the most gorgeous car, golden tan. Months after shying away from and pining for him, we ran into each other at a club owned by a mutual friend. We started dating.

We had amazing chemistry, he was super sweet, and, I swear, I was in love by about date number two. We would hang around his place, go to dinner, text all day, and, guess what else? He WOULD NOT sleep with me. We were even naked in bed a few times and he refused to put his penis in me.

Now, I was a lot younger at the time, and this had never happened to me before, and I also had never read a book like the one I've just created for you, but this situation left me mind-fucked. My self-esteem dropped. And, believe me, I just kept coming back for more. *Poor younger me!*

A year or two later we were exchanging e-mails as friends and I finally got up the nerve to ask him what had happened. And do you know what he told me? He didn't think he would satisfy me because he got so turned on when we were together that he thought he would come too quickly. Say what? You mean to tell me that I missed out on a delicious man and we never had a wedding because, in his brain, he thought he wouldn't *satisfy me*?! Yes, that's what happened. Don't make me reference grey area here again. Fine, I'm going to. This was off and on for a few years. Want to know how long I'd let myself wonder what's happening now before I'd be asking a guy what's up? A month, if he's lucky.

I've got more stories like the one above. They range from how another guy, quite recently, avoided physical intimacy because, he claimed, I was so special and in another category from other women. I'm not saying he didn't think I was great. I know he did because he'd try to see me every other day, but he'd subject me to hours of cuddling and wouldn't allow us to get to second base. He would stop us after making out for more than a few minutes. Sure, sometimes it's great to wait, and not every connection needs to turn into sex, because, as you know, sexual choices are super important for our frequency, but I don't think I need to tell you that a man who doesn't allow himself to be PG-13 with a woman after he's of a certain age just isn't normal. And, despite his efforts to use his words to trick me, I noticed he couldn't get hard. I also noticed that, when he was in his sweats, he had a small penis. And, did I care? I actually didn't. I thought he was hot and nice, but he wouldn't tell me the truth, which meant we couldn't work through it, so I stopped seeing him and told him that we needed to be friends.

I also dated a man off and on for months who I had a great time with. We're the best of friends now, but he'd conveniently fall asleep once we started getting close to being sexual. *Pause.* When we finally did get around to screwing around he'd hit orgasm in less than twenty seconds and could barely stay hard. So quickly, in fact, that we never had actual sex. And, if it couldn't have gotten more annoying, he'd pretend like it didn't happen and attempt to sext me like he had the sexual prowess of a porn star.

See where I am going with this? Don't take it personally when a guy won't allow you to get close to him while everything else is awesome. If he can't admit to you what's up, then move on. Again, you aren't there to fix him. He needs to develop maturity, learn to communicate, and possibly get on meds. It's especially important to trust yourself enough to believe in what you know to be reality. I had been naked with him. I knew what he was like in bed. He could go on pretending that he didn't have a physical problem, but I knew better, and no amount of sexting was going to make me buy what he was selling. I know this sounds ridiculous but it's gaslighting and you'll start forgetting what really happened if you let yourself. These guys will try every trick in the book to get you to believe *anything* could be happening other than the truth. So, here's the truth: He has a penis problem.

I'm not saying that if the sex isn't perfect the first time around that you need to run. In especially strong and loving connections guys can feel a lot of pressure to perform. Once they get more comfortable, they are usually fine. Aren't we happy we don't have a penis? Must be tough. Anyway, the major issue at hand here is communication. I believe that as women we tend to be understanding and loving. If a man levels with us, then we're game. This is just my view, but a guy who can be real is a guy I can respect. If he owns his penis problem, in my eyes, it's no longer a problem. And because he had balls of steel (that's a metaphor), then I'm going to love that penis come what may and have a lot of fun doing it. I might even pay for the medical bills.

Online Dating

Online dating is a tricky business and I'm a person who has a love/hate relationship with dating apps. To be a woman who can date online successfully requires extreme savvy, a "cut your losses" attitude, the ability to express oneself with grace and courage, and a thick skin.

I'll admit, because of some of the bizarre behavior I've seen from men on these apps, I have pushed against them and advised many of the women who look to me for advice to get off of dating sites.

That being said, I think we are in a very different time now. Thanks to newer apps designed by women and other ones that once had "hook-up" reputations but are now attempting to create safe environments for women with consequences for men if they don't comply, I have become a convert. But that doesn't mean you shouldn't enter without *extreme* caution and without knowing how to handle yourself.

If you think about it, how many men do you know who are flirtatious and appealing to women have problems connecting with the opposite sex organically? In my book, not many. But given that our culture has been pushed into a virtual one where guys are working from home and going out less, especially due to the recent pandemic, great guys who never found themselves needing to date online are now doing it. It's my observation that the quality of men on online dating apps has risen—*big time*—but I still maintain the belief that many men on dating sites are likely to have an aversion to relationships and intimacy or, worse, are looking to cheat. Dating apps allow these men to put a toe in the water while feeling as though a woman is interested. Many of them get their emotional needs met online because, again, women tend to get hooked into men through words and not action. *I repeat! Action is everything.* Burn it into your brain, please, because remembering this phrase is key for you not getting yourself connected to a man who isn't available. I don't want you falling in love with a robot, married man, or someone who has never figured out that developing a relationship with a woman requires him to leave his home.

I strongly advise that, when you are attempting to meet someone online, you gently prod a man you find interesting into getting off the site and into reality as quickly as possible. Being online and not talking or video chatting, or not seeing a man in person, gives him the ability to manipulate your perception of him—one that might be completely at odds with the man he really is. Love, *do not* waste your time writing to someone on a site or texting for days/weeks. Cut to the chase as quickly as possible so that you know whether or not you want to give him your valuable time and energy because, even though it's "just texting", every written exchange will pull you in emotionally. I don't want him screwing with your mind and emotions; instead, I want you to feel in control of them. *Notice that I did not say I want you in control of HIM.* We are not looking to change the dating world; we are looking to create a dynamic in your life that is selective and limited to high-quality individuals, i.e. men.

I don't like giving you a plan to follow because all men are different and I definitely handle each one differently and I also want you to be yourself, but because this realm can be difficult, I think it will be beneficial for me to walk you through how I handle online dating, so let's get started…

First, the profile. Think about why you are on the site and the kind of man you want to attract and fabricate your profile based on this notion. My pictures never have my ass to the camera or bikini shots or anything else that could give a man the idea that I'm there to meet someone for sex, looking to be arm candy, or objectified. I want my profile pictures to convey that I'm sexy, fun, smart, deep, and artsy. I like intelligent and creative men, so my photos are intentionally curated to attract this kind of man. If you're a workout buff and wanting the same kind of guy, don't you think it's important to show you lifting weights or at yoga? This is painting a picture of your interests and sending out signals to attract the same.

There is absolutely nothing wrong with you being proud of your gorgeous body. The problem with you presenting yourself in this way is that most men—because they are biologically wired for sex and lose their minds when they see a woman they desire visually— will have difficulty getting past your sexuality to know the layered and interesting woman you are. If you *must* post a shot of you in a bikini, keep it light. Maybe you're playing volleyball and having fun on the beach. This can send a message that, yes, I'm hot, but I'm also active and love the beach. Can you see the subtle difference? Here's another reason I'd prefer you not post those kinds of pictures: You can maintain some of the mystery associated with meeting you. To me, holding my allure and keeping my sexuality just out of reach, because men are natural born hunters, is a big part of the art of dating. We want him to *want* to plan that date and show up. If he doesn't, how will he ever have the chance to see you naked?

Ladies, men follow your lead. They take cues from you. They are quick to make assumptions that aren't true because, as I've already said, they *typically* have a difficult time holding binary thoughts about a woman due to men being naturally linear and having single point focus. Most men can't see you half-naked and see you as an ambitious and intelligent woman—even though you may have written on your profile that you are a rocket scientist. First, they never got to what you wrote because they were focused on your breasts. Second, they've already decided that you are going to be sending them more photos, and that fucking you is going to be as easy as: one…two…three-some. This is a slippery slope and one that can make you feel disrespected quickly.

So, here is what my profile looks like: The first shot is one of me looking fashion-forward and fun. No duck lips. I'm smiling. I have close face and full-body photos. I have black and white and color ones too. I'm careful to not post pictures that are overly filtered. My photos are cool and sexy and fun and flirty. This is, after all, who I feel that I am. I want my profile to be accurate because men who are not into me need not apply. I don't want one millisecond of my precious time wasted.

When it comes to the write-up, I keep it short. I give a quick blurb about what I do and who I am and then I end it with a question to allow the guy an entry point in starting a conversation with words other than "hi". I don't use emoticons; I use words, because I'm a grown-ass woman, but that doesn't mean if you are younger and just looking to date for fun that you shouldn't. In my write-up, I do not tell men about me emotionally or about what I'm looking for.

Here's an example of me online: "Hey! I'm artsy. I'm into business. I'm multi-faceted. I live between x and y city. What's your favorite food?" Yep, that's about it. I can feel some women gasping right now: "WTF?! That's it?!" *Yes, beauty, that's it.* To put your mind at ease, what if I told you that the large majority (about 80-90%) of the men I swipe also swipe right? Why is this as far as I go with my profile? Because, again, I'm setting myself up to be pursued. I'm keeping mystery around who I am and what I'm like; to know anything more the guy is going to have to swipe me, text me, talk to me, and then meet me.

I don't know about you, but I find incessant texting *extremely* frustrating. If I like a man, we're dating in the first two weeks, or at least talking and on video, or he's out. I'm not into being strung along for entertainment, and I don't want you ladies to be either, which is why I'm sharing some of my online dating secrets with you.

Once you get connected with a man, let him move the conversation forward. Don't over text or force getting to know him. Instead, observe his communication style and whether he's into...*you*. Does he seem genuinely interested and beyond superficial? Is he verbal, respectful, and intelligent? If he is, then I suggest you go right ahead and suggest something like the following: "I find it easier to be off this app to communicate, don't you?" If he says "no" then he's out. Most men say "yes" and understand that you aren't there to play.

We've got him off the app now and onto our phone. I should warn you some guys will suggest chatting on other apps, like WhatsApp, as the next step or even send you a message through another app without asking you, rather than texting or calling. If a guy attempts this, I ignore it for a few days and then I tell him that I'm never on there and would prefer we text. There's a good reason that I do this: Apps like the one I just named are often what married men, or men in relationships, use to keep their secret relationships (the one they might be trying to have with you) hidden. If he insists that you text on one of these apps, and it seems valid—like maybe he's in another country at the moment and it makes more sense—then I suggest you outright ask him if he's married or in a relationship. Most men will actually tell you the truth. Men in relationships will know they aren't going to get far with you when you get right to the point. If they stop texting after your question, then you have your answer and they need blocked/deleted.

After we start texting, I usually give a guy a few days of this but then suggest we video chat or I tell him something like: "You know, I'd love to see your face and hear your voice." Sometimes I will even call him off the cuff. If a man fights this with me, I move on. I know that all of this might feel pushy or masculine, but when it comes to online dating, I just see this as a necessity. I want to know what I'm dealing with. Once I do, I back off and let him start making plans. I force myself to move things into reality quickly, even though it's truly not my nature to want to be in charge of a relationship, and I do this mostly because I want to protect myself from predators, frauds, and men who are on the app for reasons other than dating and building a connection.

All of the above advice is for women who are looking for a potential relationship. If you are wanting to just have fun, then do it!! Sometimes flirting and chatting can be a great way to get your mind off of an ex without putting yourself out there. Male energy can be flattering and exciting for its own sake. Just be careful with information that you give out. Even if you're having fun, be safe. And never, I repeat, never agree to meet a man you have met online anywhere but in a public place. Don't get into a car with him. Don't go to his house. Put yourself in the driver's seat and stay there.

Last, but not least, I see dating apps as portals. I can't tell you how many times, when I used to write profiles for myself that were extensive and specific about the kind of man I wanted to meet, that I would end up meeting this exact guy offline and organically a few weeks later. I've also noticed that, when I'm online, men approach me more out in the real world. Getting online when you feel uncomfortable going out is a way to send a signal to the universe and to your higher self that you are ready and available. Taking steps online shifts your energy. Try it and have fun with it. There's a strong chance that, if you're open to the magic of it, your next boyfriend will show up non-virtually because you placed yourself in the virtual world. Energy doesn't discriminate and neither does the universe.

Break-Ups

They're hard.

Break-Ups Continued

Just kidding! Do you think I'd leave you with nothing on this subject? *Girl, please, we've got this.* Okay, but seriously, break-ups are hard. Can I get a hell yes? How many times have we let a relationship go, had some dude tell us it's not working, or given a man an ultimatum to pull his shit together just to hold onto our phone with a death grip to see if he texts a "What's up?" three days later. I write three days, maybe two and a half, because that's exactly how much time it takes before we start to panic and develop amnesia. 72 hours…that's all the time I need to forget about my anger and to remember his smile. I'll start blaming myself for every demand I ever made, asking why I have to be such a pain in the ass, and wondering how I could have possibly over-reacted to him not calling me back for five days. How could I have such high expectations? How could I possibly want that much from someone? Pause for an eye-roll.

There's no way around it, break-ups separate the real women from the weak. I've been in both categories and there are still moments when I can't believe how quickly I will give up what I want for a brief moment to feel better, despite the fact that I'm in my forties and have been through a countless number of friends, lovers, and boyfriends. I know better. To this day, I fight entering the familiar cycle I fall into after a break-up, the one where I'm my 12-year-old self who experienced rejection and was dying to feel loved, validated, and accepted. But I'm not that adolescent now, right? I'm the bomb. He knows it. I know it. *This is war.* And, for the record, that ex-12-year-old boyfriend of mine came back. Just saying.

Now, I know your friends will tell you that you were only sleeping with that guy or it hasn't been long enough for you to feel the way that you do, but I'm here to tell you that they don't know shit. How you feel is how you feel. If you fall in love in a week—*even though I don't recommend it because I don't know how in the hell you would have seen enough action from a man in that time to prove he's worthy of your love*—and that seems real to you, then it just is. And, I'm also here to tell you, even though I've warned you about "the goddess myth", that men can fall in love in a minute. Don't think they can't. I've had it happen and not just once.

They're the most emotional creatures on Earth which is why they will avoid confrontation and placing themselves in the vulnerable position of giving you the upper hand. The moment they do, they know they're fucked and in love forever. You're in control. Do you know that saying about what women and men fear most? Well, if you don't, I'm going to tell you: "Women's greatest fear is that men can kill them; men's greatest fear is that women can make them look stupid." I've taken liberty with this quote by Margaret Atwood (I'm sure she wouldn't mind.), but there's no greater chance for a man to look stupid than after a break-up. The aftermath of your split is all about who is going to have the power moving forward.

For you to survive a break-up it's absolutely crucial that you remember—tape on your refrigerator, bathroom tub, and every window of your home—the following universal law: Men are cockroaches. *MEN ARE COCKROACHES. MEN ARE COCK-ROACHES. MEN ARE COCKROACHES.* "Katie, can you please stop writing this? You're being super annoying, and it doesn't even make sense." *Men are cockroaches.* There, see how I did that? This is my book and I'll say what I like, as many times as I want, to help you. And I'll bet you're never going to forget it, which is the point. Men are cockroaches, which means, they *always* come back, whether you like it or not. *Always, always, always,* so breathe if you're currently suffering. You're welcome.

I actually think some friend of mine said this little phrase to me years ago, but I can't be sure. If she did, we owe her, because it's as reliable as the sun coming up every day. The first time I heard her say this I did an inventory of my life and thought, "OH MY GOD. She's right. How did I not realize this?" Okay, fine, ONCE! Once I had an ex not come back, but he was a unicorn, and I firmly believe it was because I didn't have the patience and knowledge of this golden rule and acted way too quickly after he decided to shell-shock me by telling me he didn't want to be in a relationship anymore. He's the one and only man in my life who ever broke up with me. I fell apart. It fucked with my head, mostly because, at the time, I felt I was out of his league.

Let me tell you how important it is that you handle a break-up like a champ. It's vital to your self-confidence and general well-being. You know that kid I just mentioned? Well, I can tell you that before I met him rejection didn't enter my mind (except when I was a kid). He screwed with my self-esteem. My ego was so damaged that it took me almost ten years to get it back. So, can you see that break-ups are about much more than you losing the guy? Of course we want to see him return. We want YOU making the choices, but, most of all, we want you feeling good a year from now. In a year you're probably not going to remember the guy's name who just broke your heart, but, unfortunately, you might find him camping out in your medulla oblongata if you gave your power away. I think we both know that no man deserves that from you.

Katie wanted me to tell you here how to get your power back, but that's not the point, because we don't want to get it back. I mean, we can, but that's tough and also not guaranteed. What we want is to never lose it. And how we hold on to it is by standing our ground, not reaching out, and letting him come back ON HIS OWN, because the universal law of *men are cockroaches* has a catch: We don't know when he's coming back. It could be days, weeks, or months. Yes, darling, a break-up often requires you to have metaphoric balls of steel and the mental strength of Gandhi. So, how are you going to get through this? Any fucking way you can, that's how.

I realize that therapists and all those other dating and self-help books are going to tell you to use this time to be your best self and to get to the gym. Are they fucking serious? Do they have ice running through their veins? Let me give you some advice you can actually use. Do whatever you can to get through the day in the beginning. It's one day at a time here. The break-up I shared with you had me doing nothing but eating (barely), sleeping, working, crying in the shower, and drinking bottles of wine. I did that for two months. Sometimes I drank wine in the shower *while* crying. You know Tove Lo's song *Habits*?

That's basically me after a break-up, but does he know that? Fuck no, he doesn't. For all he knows I'm dating someone else and not giving him a second thought. Some days are going to feel easy; you're going to make it to the gym and maybe even paint your apartment.

Others are going to require that you lock your cell phone in a drawer so that you don't make a call, send a song or picture, or text a general "I fucking hate you" message. Send those text messages to your BFF. Sometimes all you need to do is express yourself and relieve your mind of toxic thoughts, so put them into words and send them, just not to him. Ask your girlfriend to send you a sweet reply in response as if she's him. You wouldn't believe how healthy this exercise can be for your suffering psyche and a heart that's on the mend. Also, if you're coming off a fresh break, be mindful if you're going to be drinking. Give your phone to your friend. It's just too tempting for you to lose your mind for a moment. Trust me, you're going to hate yourself in the morning. Ballers don't become ballers by caving. *Get tough.*

Let's talk about some other things you're going to do. I'm going to allow you ONE weekend to talk about that asshole, and then you're done. You heard me, ONE weekend. That's two days in case you aren't doing the math because he doesn't deserve your energy and also because you're hearing yourself and so is the universe. Are you trying to call the same bullshit into your life? Talk like a badass. Make every effort to go out and look amazing when you're ready. Eventually, you're going to believe what you hear and see.

While we're at it, I'm going to remind you here to be careful who you talk to. If you hear one friend tell you that you made a mistake, you're going to question yourself. Talk to the friends who have your back and take your side no matter what the cost. Talk to your mom if it makes sense. I don't care. Just don't talk to your friends who are weak-ass, ultra-compassionate fairy children who want to give you his side of this. You can turn to them when you're rearing your children. I have a friend whom I love who does this very thing. She is a doll. But nothing irritates me more than when we are talking about one of our girlfriends and she starts taking the side of the guy. Do you know what I say to her when she does this? "I don't care how flawed our friend is. Her ex has his own friends. They worry about him. We worry about her." See how that works? And if you are that friend, check yourself. Your girlfriend has enough questions going through her mind without you trying to play analyst.

Timelines are important, so I would invite you to make an attempt to get level after week one. I'm giving you week one to act crazy, break things, stalk his social media, and to cry yourself to sleep. Go to bed with a picture of him and make out with it for all I care; just don't let him—or his friends—know. It's important to allow your feelings. Do it! Indulge yourself. But after week one, try and take a deep breath.

 Emotions run up and down, so if you're super angry try to calm yourself. If you feel depressed go have a coffee. Try to turn the stories off in your head, starting now. Meditation is amazing for just bringing yourself back to you, which is where your attention ideally should turn after week one. This doesn't mean you're not going to suffer. This is a tough time. But staying as even keel as possible is important for you to feel good, and feeling good is where it's at. I have this nasty habit of turning into a control freak at work when I'm feeling hurt in my personal life. I basically become Hitler, so know your patterns and that it's not the job of the people who love you to deal with your bullshit just because he isn't. I know this about myself, so I try to keep an awareness about my own behavior, not just for those I care about, but because I deserve more than to punish myself by making other parts of my life harder than they have to be.

If I feel tempted to reach out, I like to invent little challenges for myself. One of my favorites is to give myself a goal of the number of days not to contact him. My ideal number is twenty-one. It takes twenty-one days to typically break, or create, a habit. And I've definitely noticed that after week three I become particularly in control of my feelings and he starts to fade. I like to promise myself rewards when I get this far. Make sure it's something you really want and wouldn't normally give yourself. I've done this in the past but the last break-up I went through I gave myself a major reward when he contacted me. I just said, it's all or nothing. I put the name of a jewelry designer as a replacement of his name in my cell phone. Every time I looked at his number or thought about reaching out I was reminded of the piece of jewelry I was going to have if I didn't. You can give yourself something for every week you make it. Or don't. Just remember, break-up survival is truly about tricking your mind and giving yourself reminders of why you aren't taking the easy way out and re-connecting.

"Goodness, Katie, the games you play." *Is that what you are thinking? That this is a game? Wrong. This is your life.* It's one shot, baby, and you deserve to be loved. But do you know what else? Your guy deserves the opportunity to show his best self. You're doing this for the both of you. He has earned the right not to be told what to do or to be helped along by you. He wants a woman to love. He wants a woman who is strong. You're both winning. And why would you want to deny yourself the chance to be shown that someone can genuinely step up for you? Believe it. If he loves you, or just desires you, he can and will. If the relationship picks back up, it will be more solid because he won you and you also respected yourself. No person who cares for you would ever want you to dilute yourself so much that you feel badly. This man will also know you are no woman to take for granted. Take my word for it, he wants nothing more than to meet that woman, and that woman is you.

The problem with break-ups is that we forget where our happiness came from in the first place, and this next concept was once pointed out to me by a coach of mine. He told me that the magnificent physical and chemical connection I thought I had with my ex was actually an energy that I created, one that couldn't have been there without *me*. If this man were to be with another woman, the dynamic couldn't and wouldn't exist. I know this sounds like inaccessible idealism, but it isn't, so once you've calmed yourself enough to come back into grounded reality, where your feelings aren't fresh and magnified, it's important that you focus on this concept: *You are required to be present for the love you had.*

The man who just left your life—for whatever reason and whoever's choice it was—is now absent because there was a problem, right? It's very rare that a relationship or connection alleviates itself when frequencies are matched. Both people want the same thing. They want to be together. And if that's present for both people where is it really going? Nowhere.

Doll, let me remind you again, his is *not* the last penis on earth. This is *not* the last time you are going to love. You—no one else—are the creator of your life and the universe has to match your energy. Once I had a 72-year-old woman whose husband had passed only a few years prior walk into my office and very excitedly tell my staff and me about a man she had just met online. He had flown to see her from another part of the country so that they could spend the weekend together. Very recently, I met another woman while I was out dancing one evening. She was sixty-five. And let me tell you I had to take a deep breath because this chick was hot. She was smoking hot at sixty-five. I couldn't believe she wasn't in her early forties. She and I got into a very deep discussion about dating. She had left her husband three years before. She was so happy to be single and was attempting to figure out the dating world just like the rest of us. How cool is that?

I'm telling you these stories because, for some reason, every woman on earth, including me, starts to convince herself that she has to settle because she accessed 60% of the person she truly wanted. You don't. YOU created the energy with that man. Don't kid yourself, you also attracted this person to you and called him in because of what lives inside of you. And you will do it again, but better, if his frequency doesn't shift. Yes, he will reach out to you eventually, because, what did I tell you?! *Men are cockroaches*. But that doesn't mean he's your guy. He might come back just to test the waters or because he misses you like crazy and is now convinced you are the one, but he just can't up-level. You have to decide what you want and what it is that you deserve. The world is your oyster, dear.

There's one additional thing you need to know about break-ups. Sometimes, they're a normal step couples go through to survive. I've been in very few long-term relationships where I didn't have to walk away in the first month or two. It usually happens after everyone's had a lot of sex and the time of their lives and the relationship transitions from peaches and cream-land into reality.

And most of the time, it's because your guy doesn't realize that, just because you love him, you're not going to be taken for granted. *Sorry to report this, ladies.* Sure, there is the occasional man—usually over fifty and very adult—who knows better. He's fucked up so many times in relationships that he's not going to let his ego get the better of him. Or, maybe you're lucky enough to have a man who *needs* his chick happy for him to be happy, so you're not required to pass through the break-up phase. But, for the most part, temporary splits have to happen for power dynamics, so don't get discouraged. Keep it moving. Chances are that you're going to go one or two rounds before your connection stabilizes and gets real or finally fizzles out. Try not to lose your mind in the process.

Farewell, Katie

Well, beauty, I've given you some of my best stuff so it's time for me to say goodbye and wish you well. Go out there and enjoy yourself. Try to remember that nothing in this life is about attaining a goal or getting a man. Everyone we meet is just here to get us closer to our own truth. Some people come into our lives to teach us lessons; others come to us to support us or to create friendships that may last a lifetime. Most of the time we don't know the difference. I sincerely believe we are, despite what we are told, here to grow and to become our best selves, so try not to take it all so seriously. Find a way to love life because it's so very precious. Enjoy every day like it's your last damn day here. Be courageous in life and in love. Be brave enough to find and be yourself.

Oh, and just in case you're wondering, Katie is now in a wonderful, committed relationship...her first-ever. She also just gave birth to a baby boy.

I love you, Katie.

Acknowledgments

I would be remiss if I didn't specifically thank Nicola Humber for this book. She's one of the coaches mentioned and also the woman who agreed to publish my work. Nicola, you are a fucking gift!!! Thank you for holding the space for me to be me and for encouraging me to wade through this information when I wanted to give up.

I also want to thank Christelle Chopard, Rebecca Steiger, and Brandon Olivares for all the time and energy that they devoted to my growth over the years and for leading me here.

Thank you to Glenda (She knows who she is.) for spending hours on end helping me to edit this book and to all my friends who encouraged me to create *This is for Katie*. Sharing one's own stories and opinions, it seems, is much more intimidating than ever becoming a doctor.

Most of all I want to thank all the wonderful men who have been in my life. You have been my greatest teachers...

About the Unbound Press

The Unbound Press is a soul-led publishing imprint committed to working with female authors whose work activates a feeling of deep connection and transformation in others.

Movements such as #MeToo have shown us the power of women coming together and sharing their stories. And if there's one thing we're certain of, it's that in these times, the world NEEDS your magic.

We honour the right of all beings to be their most free selves and to write from that place. We truly believe that we can change the world, one book at a time. Are you in?

Find out more at: **theunboundpress.com**